THE BAJA CALIFORNIA COOKBOOK

THE BAJA CALIFORNIA COOKBOOK

EXPLORING THE GOOD LIFE IN MEXICO

David Castro Hussong
& Jay Porter

Photographs by Oriana Koren

TEN SPEED PRESS
California | New York

contents

WELCOME TO
BAJA

To get to my restaurant, Fauna, from the United States, you'll probably drive south from San Diego and through the busiest overland border crossing in the world.

From there, you'll skirt the chaotic, hip melting pot of Tijuana and get on the highway that runs along the coast. For an hour, you'll encounter a procession of fishing villages and housing developments, sheer cliffs and inviting shorelines.

When you are safely past a bay named Salsipuedes—Spanish for "Get out if you can"—you'll turn inland to find yourself, almost immediately, in Mexico's most notable wine-growing region, the Valle de Guadalupe. At the end of a dirt road lined with hundred-year-old olive trees, you'll park, walk up a gravel path, and be here.

The first people to live on this land were the Kumiai, who arrived twelve thousand years ago; their descendants still live a couple miles from this spot, in the community of San Antonio Necua. Meanwhile, the historical presence of the Spanish, who planted our initial grapevines centuries ago, resonates in the Valle, as it does throughout Mexico.

It was a group of Russian emigrants in the 1920s, however, who really made this area into a wine region. They were called Molokans, and they owned most of the Valle then. I've been told that Russian was the default language even into the 1950s. You still meet people here with Russian names, and you still see shops that bake and sell Russian bread.

Over a couple generations, others came, including industrial winemakers along with the farmers and workers they require. Eventually, almost all of Mexico's domestic wine came from this region. Most of it was inexpensive, anodyne, and made according to the principles of large-scale production.

About thirty years ago, a new wave of people became prominent in the Valle, people with ideas to explore its potential for world-class wine and food. Among them were winemakers, chefs, artists, and even the architect who designed the winery and restaurant where I cook.

———

It's 7 a.m. when the dogs wake me up. I take them down along the beach, the same beach I grew up walking along. Maribel, who I've been with since we were teens, is still sleeping.

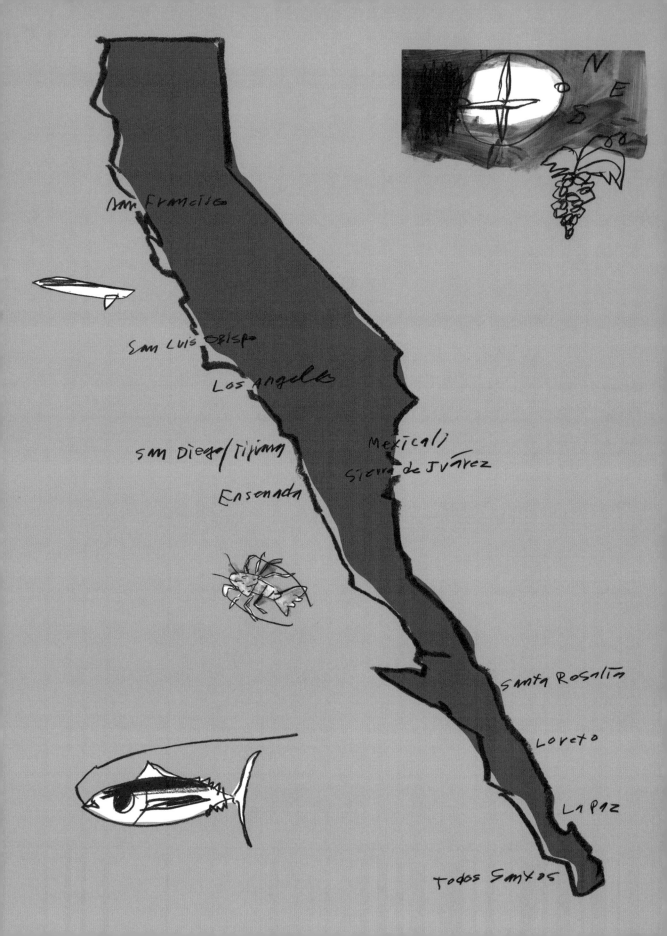

San Francisco

San Luis Obispo

Los Angeles

San Diego/Tijuana

Ensenada

Mexicali
Sierra de Juárez

Santa Rosalía

Loreto

La Paz

Todos Santos

N
E
S
O

I head downtown for some morning coffee at Barra D' Café. It's one of Ensenada's newest coffee purveyors. Barra D' Café roasts very small batches of Mexican coffee in the former home of Santo Tomas, which is one of California's oldest wineries.

After having coffee, I walk a couple doors down to a little fresh-fish shop called De Garo, to pick up culinary seaweed from Japan, and maybe some local seaweed. Next door at Mercados El Roble, I buy some chickens for that night's staff dinner, as well as some specialties from the United States that the owner is kind enough to import for me.

If it's a Sunday, I'll drive a few blocks to the harbor and its public fish market, which is named Mercado Negro ("Black Market"). My distributors don't deliver to the restaurant on Sundays; but at the dockside market, I can buy from the guy who sells to my distributors anyway. I pick up *jurel* (known in the United States as yellowtail jack or hamachi), oysters, and some chocolate clams or blood clams.

Many people have read Anthony Bourdain's book *Kitchen Confidential*, in which he warns against ordering seafood on Sundays and Mondays in New York City restaurants. Some people think that his advice is relevant in every city in the world. Not true! Around here, weekend fish is super. Local *panga* boats—a kind of fishing skiff invented in Baja—bring in a catch on Saturday evening, which gets readied for sale just in time for Sunday morning. And then, early on Monday morning, the local aqua farms bring in their product, so we have great fish on Mondays, too.

Every morning after my errands are done, I try to sneak in some time at the gym. And I'll probably try to take care of a few more errands, too. Like, I might swing by my uncle's warehouse to pick up some wine. Or if I'm low on mezcal, I'll go to a specialty store that's located in nearby San Dieguito ("Little San Diego"), where it's hidden in with the Costco and other big-box stores.

By the time I arrive at Fauna, it's probably around 2 p.m., meaning we've been open for a little while already. In Mexico, lunch is the big dining-out meal, even during the week, so our team is probably as busy as we're going to be all day.

The first thing I do is make sure we are keeping the fridge well organized because organization is the first step to creating great food! Then I get to it: tasting, checking, helping, cooking, serving, and making sure all our guests are happy and well-fed. I've been doing this work since I was in middle school; my family's been doing it for well over a century, here on the Pacific coast of Baja California.

My mom's family is well-known in Baja and in Southern California. Her grandfather John Hussong founded a bar, called Hussong's Cantina, in Ensenada in 1892, and it is still open today. We think it's the oldest continuously operating bar in all the Californias. People on both sides of the border have good memories of hanging out at Hussong's, with its peanut shells on the floor, old newspaper clippings on the walls, and mariachis leading the crowd in sing-alongs. It's even thought to be the place where the margarita was invented!

In every generation after John, many Hussongs have worked in the food and hospitality business. My grandfather was kicked out of his house as a young man—it's a long story—and he moved

about a mile out from downtown Ensenada to a place on the beach near where I grew up. There he caught lobsters and sold them at a profit to businesses in the United States. At that time, contraband liquor sales to the States was a booming trade—it was during Prohibition—and I've seen a photograph of my grandfather with Al Capone, so it may be that there was more than just lobsters in those crates. But the live Baja lobsters were definitely there, too. And they were—and still are—delicious.

More recently, my uncle Carlos operated a tuna fleet based on the same stretch of beach until the early 1990s, when the *embargo atunero*—the effective ban on commercial tuna fishing methods in both Californias—put an end to the industry here. Now, if you go to that spot, you'll find a steakhouse and bar run by my cousin. And in the early 2000s, my uncle Juan Antonio was the chef at Punto Morro hotel, a nice beachfront place near our house.

Around that time, I was thirteen years old, and my mom asked me, in the way that moms do, what I planned to do with my life. "I'm going to be a chef," I told her. I loved food and had watched my family cooking with intention since I could remember. Of course I, too, would do that. She called Juan Antonio and told him he had a new *pinche*. After that, all through high school, I spent my weekends chopping onions and learning how to cook professionally from Juan Antonio's sous chefs.

During the week, when I was in school, my dad worked down the road as a university professor. He taught anthropology, sociology, and urban planning. His family never opened a bar—so they are not famous like the Hussongs—but they've been in California longer. If I have a claim that I'm an old-school *Californio*, it's through them. Long ago, they were farmers in Santa Rosalia, a ranching and mining town about halfway down the Baja peninsula. In time, my dad's dad moved to the Sierras of northern Baja and acquired his own ranchland in the mountains, raising cattle and lambs. That land is still in our family, and neighboring farmers use it for pasturing their animals.

When I was eighteen, I left Baja to pursue my career. It's a funny thing; I tried my hand in a good Italian restaurant in San Diego, where I worked as a pizzaiolo. I hated it for no particular reason—it was a perfectly good place to cook—and ended up working there for not long at all, maybe a month or two. And then I quit, came back to Ensenada, and took Maribel out for a drink to celebrate moving home. At the bar, I ran into my friend and previous boss, chef Jair Téllez of Laja, who was about to open his first restaurant in Mexico City. The next thing I knew, I was packing up my knives again.

Over the following few years, I cooked in Mexico City, San Diego, Copenhagen, and New York. Twice—working at Eleven Madison Park and staging at Noma—I found myself in kitchens in the top five of the "World's Best Restaurants" list. Two more times I worked at restaurants that have been on the "50 Best" list for Latin America. I settled in as a chef in San Francisco for a couple years, before getting an offer to helm a restaurant that would be my own. In a fun twist, the new restaurant was next to my hometown, in the Guadalupe Valley wine country outside Ensenada.

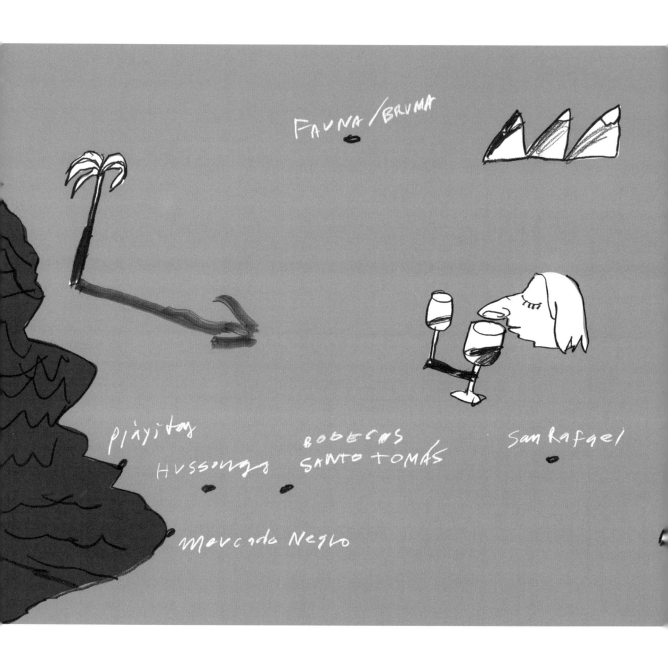

Castro Family Ranch

If you drive through the Guadalupe Valley, it looks very similar to the wine country of Sonoma, or the one near Santa Barbara. And if you go up higher, into the Sierra de Juarez near my father's family's ranch, you could easily be in any of the mountains of Southern California.

A lot of people know about "California Cuisine," an idea to cook in a European style using super-local ingredients. This movement started in Berkeley in the 1970s and spread like wildfire. Even now, it is more or less required in the Bay Area to understand this kind of cooking in order to work in an accomplished restaurant kitchen.

Of course, there's another, related, kind of "California Cuisine," and that's what this book is about. This is cooking that, in one form or another, used to happen in the whole of California, from Los Cabos and Loreto all the way up to Monterey and San Francisco and Mendocino. A cuisine that also combined the bounty of the Pacific with Old World staples such as olive oil, wheat, wine grapes, and ranch meats.

North of the border, the more modern version of this cuisine has fully supplanted the historic one, but Baja's food culture has changed at a less overwhelming pace. And, to the extent that it has reshaped itself, this has often occurred along vectors that are unique, sometimes surprising, and occasionally downright avant-garde. The result is a style of cooking and eating that is both rooted in hundreds of years of life here but also full of fresh new approaches.

One idea, of course, stays the same on both sides of the line— the golden promise of California, projected onto the place by each generation of arrivals since Spanish sailors first lit upon Cedros Island. They thought they had discovered *California*, a fictional island described in a popular novel of the time as "very close to the side of the Earthly Paradise." The idea that this is a place of plenty—of sunshine, of flowers and fruit, of pearls and gold—still captivates our imaginations. Whether it's inspired by Hollywood or *Sunset* magazine, we think of California as a land of sea breezes and backyard barbecues, with the best of wine country and beach living rolled into one.

And this image, I think in most of our minds, includes a lot of delicious food.

The recipes in this book are mostly simple to execute,* and the resulting dishes are not fancy or pretentious. It's all suitable for a weeknight dinner at home, for grilling on your patio some Sunday afternoon when friends drop by, or, for that matter, a bonfire wedding reception on the beach with longneck beers and a makeshift bocce ball game. It's all about just enjoying this place we all, on both sides of the border, call California.

David C.

* The main exception: Learning to make flour tortillas—which is, in some ways, a foundational recipe of this book—can take some time and practice for the uninitiated to master. But don't worry if you aren't immediately an expert; a freshly baked sourdough baguette from your local market makes a perfectly good substitute.

AT THE RANCH

Many of us who grew up in Baja, even fairly recently, have a connection to ranches and farms; for generations, those were at the center of people's lives here. While the texture of Baja life has changed a lot in the last few decades, the food we eat is still influenced by Spanish-flavored ranch culture.

For almost twenty thousand years, indigenous people had the peninsula to themselves. Then, in the 1600s, colonizers flying the Spanish flag established their first mission in Loreto, on the Sea of Cortez in what now is the state of Baja California Sur. These missionaries, in order to better control California's land and people, asked Spain to send ranchers to establish farms.

Many of those first Spanish ranchers were from the south of Spain and had Moorish heritage. People say they brought Bedouin hospitality traditions with them, which are still present in Baja's small mountain villages. It's tough to prove this conclusively, but what we can show is that they did bring with them their Mediterranean larder, including olives, wine grapes, dates, cattle, and wheat for flour. These were the original cultivated crops of the California ranch, and they are still being farmed here today.

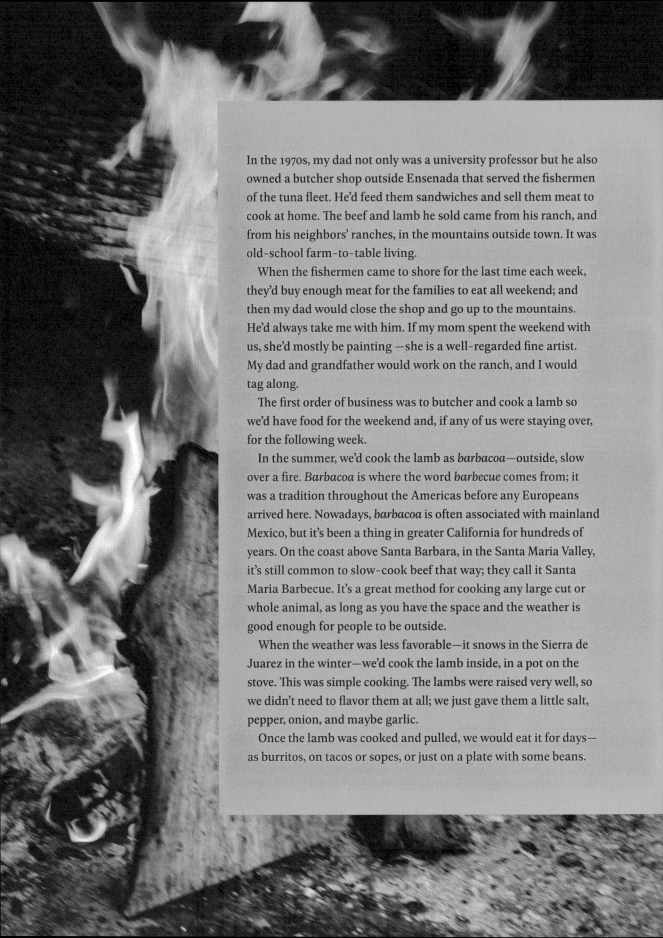

In the 1970s, my dad not only was a university professor but he also owned a butcher shop outside Ensenada that served the fishermen of the tuna fleet. He'd feed them sandwiches and sell them meat to cook at home. The beef and lamb he sold came from his ranch, and from his neighbors' ranches, in the mountains outside town. It was old-school farm-to-table living.

When the fishermen came to shore for the last time each week, they'd buy enough meat for the families to eat all weekend; and then my dad would close the shop and go up to the mountains. He'd always take me with him. If my mom spent the weekend with us, she'd mostly be painting —she is a well-regarded fine artist. My dad and grandfather would work on the ranch, and I would tag along.

The first order of business was to butcher and cook a lamb so we'd have food for the weekend and, if any of us were staying over, for the following week.

In the summer, we'd cook the lamb as *barbacoa*—outside, slow over a fire. *Barbacoa* is where the word *barbecue* comes from; it was a tradition throughout the Americas before any Europeans arrived here. Nowadays, *barbacoa* is often associated with mainland Mexico, but it's been a thing in greater California for hundreds of years. On the coast above Santa Barbara, in the Santa Maria Valley, it's still common to slow-cook beef that way; they call it Santa Maria Barbecue. It's a great method for cooking any large cut or whole animal, as long as you have the space and the weather is good enough for people to be outside.

When the weather was less favorable—it snows in the Sierra de Juarez in the winter—we'd cook the lamb inside, in a pot on the stove. This was simple cooking. The lambs were raised very well, so we didn't need to flavor them at all; we just gave them a little salt, pepper, onion, and maybe garlic.

Once the lamb was cooked and pulled, we would eat it for days—as burritos, on tacos or sopes, or just on a plate with some beans.

Serves 4 to 20, depending
on how many tortillas and
beans you put next to it

Braised lamb, ranch-style

2 to 3 pounds lamb (either bone-in or boneless is fine)

1 yellow onion, peeled and quartered

6 to 8 garlic cloves (unpeeled)

Kosher salt (see Note)

For serving

Flour tortillas (see page 38), or sourdough baguette (optional)

Basic Beans (page 51; optional)

Tomatillo/Avocado Sauce (page 78)

The following method, adjusted for scale, is how we cook whole lambs at the restaurant, but it works well for any amount of meat. If you have a specialty butcher, you can probably get leg, shoulder, or neck; all of those are good cuts for braising. I'd recommend against buying loins and chops for slow-cooking; those cuts are more expensive and cooking them on the grill will show them off better.

At the ranch, we used a huge stockpot because we'd be cooking dozens of pounds of meat, but for 2 to 3 pounds, a roasting pan or Dutch oven will be sufficiently large.

Note: Use 3 tablespoons salt per 1 pound of lamb when seasoning.

If the lamb is in a net, cut off and discard the net. Put the lamb on the bottom of a roasting pan or Dutch oven. Add the onion and garlic and fill the pan with water until the lamb is covered.

Add salt to the pan.

Cover the roasting pan and bake at 350°F for 8 hours, until the lamb is so tender it's falling apart (and falling off the bone, if there is one). Periodically check that the liquid does not evaporate completely (top it off with hot water from a kettle if needed).

When the lamb is finished cooking, use a wire spoon or mesh strainer to pull the meat from the pot. (To conserve the broth for use in another recipe, such as Lamb Ravioli in Jus, page 223, strain it into a container and refrigerate or freeze.) Discard the remaining contents of the pot.

You can store the lamb in the fridge for a couple days or serve it immediately with flour tortillas, beans, and tomatillo/avocado sauce. Or just eat it out of a bowl with your fingers.

Before each of our Friday drives to the ranch, my dad would put a few burritos together for us to eat on the ride. Now, what we call burritos in Mexico aren't the same thing you get when you order a burrito in the States. Those big stuffed pillows with tucked-in ends, like you get at Chipotle or even just across the border from Baja in San Diego, were invented in the United States, and you don't really see them anywhere in Mexico. Instead, what we call a burrito is a small flour tortilla (usually 6 to 8 inches in diameter), rolled around a simple filling, often meat. The ends stay open, not folded.

When we were leaving for the mountains, my dad would make, say, a dozen burritos, and we'd keep them warm, wrapped in tin foil, for our drive. The idea was that we'd eat them for dinner after we arrived at the ranch, and maybe even for lunch the next day. But when you're riding in the car, and the aroma of the burritos keeps smacking you in the face—well, I don't know if we ever made it all the way to the ranch before eating a full meal's worth.

These burritos were filled with beef—specifically *machaca*, and sometimes with *machaca con huevos* (machaca with scrambled eggs). Machaca is the most common burrito filling in Baja; I think if you see a sign for "burritos" on a roadside food stand, it's pretty much always going to be machaca.

Machaca is real-deal Western ranch food. It's made from dried beef that is rehydrated; in the process, its flavor gets intensified. It tastes a little like it's been spiced, but actually the meat itself has just developed its own strong character.

In the old days, you'd take sliced beef—usually a lean, cheaper cut—pound it thin, salt it heavily, and hang it outside in the sun and wind to dry. Once the beef dried, you could store it without refrigeration. It would be similar to beef jerky, but typically this machaca beef was thin sliced or shredded.

More recently, cooks might dry the beef by slicing it thin, salting it, and slow-cooking it in a dry pan to concentrate the flavors.

When it's time to rehydrate the machaca, a typical method is to slowly cook tomatoes and onions in a pan, along with the beef. The beef takes in the liquid from the tomatoes and eventually breaks down into a kind of stew.

Beef machaca with eggs

1 tablespoon neutral cooking oil, such as canola oil

1 red onion, peeled and diced

2 tomatoes, stemmed and diced

3 serrano chiles, diced

½ teaspoon kosher salt

6 ounces dried beef

6 eggs

For serving

Refried beans (see page 32)

Grated Cotija cheese

Charred Green Salsa (page 31)

Machaca con huevos is a breakfast staple not just in Baja but throughout northern Mexico. It's great in a burrito, and you'll also encounter it, as in this recipe, served on a plate alongside beans and tortillas. The photograph opposite is a version from restaurant Pan Que Pan in Loreto, Baja California Sur.

To make machaca at home, it's easiest (while still being very authentic) to start with a packaged dried beef product called *carne seca*. Many U.S. cities, both big and small, have Mexican markets that sell specialty items like this. If you don't have access to a market or if just prefer doing the recipe from scratch, you can use our method for drying beef on page 34.

Note: This recipe works well with any type of tomato that you have on hand.

Warm the cooking oil in a large cast-iron or nonstick skillet over medium-low heat. Add the onion and let it cook until it softens and becomes slightly translucent, about 5 minutes.

Add the tomatoes to the skillet and continue to cook until they soften, about 5 minutes more. Add the chiles. If the mixture starts to dry out any time during cooking, add a small amount of hot water from the tap.

Sprinkle the salt over the contents of the pan.

After about 10 minutes—once the chiles have softened and the tomatoes have started to release their liquid—add the dried beef. Cook, stirring periodically, until the beef has absorbed some of the liquid and has a juicy texture, 20 to 30 minutes. If you need more liquid in the pan to reconstitute the beef, add hot water a little at a time. Cover the pan as needed to keep the moisture in so the mixture doesn't dry out. Be sure to keep the heat low so the meat doesn't crisp onto the pan.

Once the beef has become stewy, turn the heat to medium. Crack the eggs directly into the pan and stir vigorously. As the eggs scramble, they will start taking on some of the colors of the other food in the pan. When they are fully cooked, they will still be moist, but they'll have a little firmness and the whites and yolks will no longer be translucent at all. This might take only a couple of minutes. As soon as the eggs have cooked, remove the whole pan from the heat.

Serve the machaca accompanied by refried beans topped with grated Cotija cheese and green salsa.

Charred green salsa

---

12 ounces tomatillos, husked, stemmed, and cleaned

2 serrano chiles, stemmed

1 garlic clove, peeled

1 yellow onion, peeled and cut into eighths

Kosher salt

Lime juice for serving

Salsa is a Spanish word for "sauce." In the United States, salsas are often paired with chips, but in Mexican cuisine different salsas are used for different purposes; a salsa meant to add some punch to a mild dish might be too spicy to use as a dip. This salsa, for instance, can be pretty spicy. You can make it less hot if you remove the ribs and seeds from the serrano chiles before cooking them. Remember to wear gloves when handling chiles, and do not touch your face.

In a very hot pan, or over a grill, char the tomatillos, chiles, garlic, and onion. Try to get the tomatillo skins dark and blistered, without drying out the inside or letting all the internal juices escape. It can be hard to make that all happen; don't worry if it isn't perfect.

In a blender or food processor, puree all the charred ingredients. Season with salt and lime juice. Green salsa will keep in the fridge for up to 1 week.

Refried beans

¼ cup lard or vegetable oil

1 large yellow onion, peeled and diced

½ pound dried beans, cooked according to Basic Beans (page 51), along with their liquor

Kosher salt

First things first: Refried beans aren't actually fried twice. The name "refried" is a sloppy translation of the Spanish *refrito*, which in this case is used to indicate something more along the idea of "sautéed until well-done." The idea is to heat already cooked beans in fat, while also mashing them into a paste as their liquor evaporates.

This recipe works equally well with many types of beans, including black beans, pinto beans, pink beans, and pinquito beans. I usually make refried beans from black beans, but there is no "right" answer for this cuisine. It is great to experiment and find what you like best.

Melt the lard in a large pan over medium heat. (You want the lard hot enough so that the onion will sizzle a little when added to the pan but not so hot that the lard smokes.) Add the onion and cook slowly, stirring as needed to keep it from sticking to the bottom of the pan, until the onion is translucent and yellow tinted, about 5 minutes.

Turn the heat to medium-high, wait a minute for the pan to heat up, and then use a slotted spoon or strainer to add the beans to the pan. Keep the bean liquor handy for adding later as needed. Stirring regularly, cook until the beans are very tender; depending on the beans this may take anywhere from 10 minutes to 45 minutes. Cover the pan if necessary to keep the heat and moisture in the pan. If the beans dry out too much, add a little of the bean liquor (or water, if you don't have the bean liquor for whatever reason). Once the beans have fully softened, but before removing the pan from the heat, mash the beans softly with a wooden spoon so they congeal into a putty-like consistency. Then remove the pan from the heat.

Season the beans with salt and serve.

ON DRY-COOKING
BEEF FOR MACHACA

Drying out beef for machaca at home is pretty easy, because—unlike making jerky—you'll be storing it in the fridge or freezer, so you don't have to worry about drying it to the point where it's safe to store at room temperature. In fact, it's a little better if you don't fully dry out the beef when making machaca, because then it will reconstitute more quickly when you are finishing it in the pan.

Machaca is typically made with cheaper cuts, nothing fancy. You can use any lean piece of beef. (Meat with too much fat is difficult to dry out evenly.)

The most important part of preparing the beef for machaca is to get it sliced very thin, as though you're making carpaccio.

To easily slice it thin, you can use the same method that home cooks use for making sashimi. Take the beef, wrap it in plastic wrap, and put it in the freezer just long enough that it hardens but not so long that it is thoroughly frozen (some cooks call this par-freezing, where *par* is short for "partially"). For a small piece of beef in a home freezer, this will probably take about 3 hours.

Pull out the beef, unwrap it, and then use a good chef's knife to cut off very thin slices. If the beef is frozen to the right level and your knife is sharp, it should be easy to slice thin. You can also use a mandolin to cut the beef, which makes for beautifully delicate slices, but when you use a mandolin, it is notoriously difficult not to cut your fingers, too.

After you cut the beef thin, generously salt the slices on both sides. Use a lot of salt. Don't worry if tastes a little too salty after it's dried, some of the saltiness will soak out into the liquid when you reconstitute the beef.

To dry the beef, you can either (1) cook it, with no oil, in a seasoned cast iron or nonstick pan over very low heat, or (2) lay it on roasting racks over sheet pans and cook it in the oven for no more than 3 hours at the lowest heat your oven will hold but no lower than 200°F. You can also dry it in the oven directly on sheet pans (with no roasting racks), but you'll have to take the pan out after the meat has started drying, knock the pieces around so they don't stick to the pan, and then return the pan to the oven.

Dry-cook the beef like this until it is pretty dry and just the slightest bit tender; the meat should be dry enough that you can easily tear it by hand but not so dry that it just crumbles. This might take 30 minutes in a pan on the stove, or a couple hours in the oven.

Once the meat has been dried, remove it from the heat to cool. After it has cooled enough to comfortably work with, use a knife to sliver the beef, aiming for pieces about 1 inch long. (It's fine if you have a lot of variation in length, though.)

Use the pieces right away in the machaca recipe or store them in the fridge until you need them. (They'll keep for 1 week if wrapped tightly.)

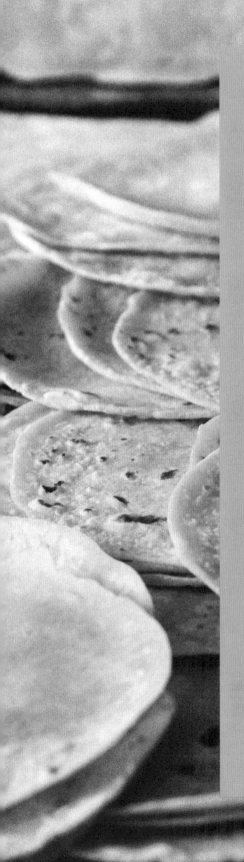

If one food ties together all of Baja California, I think it's the flour tortilla. A lot of times, a Baja meal is just one simple dish of a few good ingredients, cooked thoughtfully, served alongside fresh-made flour tortillas.

Californios have been growing wheat and making flour tortillas for more than three centuries. Meanwhile, tortillas made from corn—which is not a widely cultivated crop in Baja California—became common here only about sixty years ago. Flour tortillas are part of daily life in Baja in a way that you don't see in much of mainland Mexico.

Growing up in Ensenada, we would usually buy our tortillas from a stand almost underneath the bridge on 11th Street, alongside the concrete riverbank. More or less every town in Baja has a place like this where you can buy really delicious tortillas. Even in the tiny villages in the mountains, you'll see small shops with signs for "*tortillas de harina*," flour tortillas. Sometimes even the most unassuming restaurants and taco stands will make flour tortillas by hand, to order.

The most important thing with flour tortillas is that they be fresh made. You've got to eat them when they are still warm from being cooked! You buy or make the tortillas in the afternoon and eat them with dinner before they've fully cooled off. By the next day, they're stale and unusable, and all you can do is throw them out.

I think that flour tortillas sold in the States are nothing like what we eat in Baja, because fresh-made tortillas don't keep. U.S. towns don't usually have a little tortilla shop that everyone goes to every day; instead when you go to a supermarket, you find these kind of plastic tortilla-like things that can last on the shelf for days or even weeks. It's a totally different food.

Maybe once or twice I've discovered a small producer in the United States making the fresh kind of flour tortilla, but that's so rare that for most people north of the border, it's more practical to just make your own. It's not complex, and the recipe calls for only four ingredients. It sometimes takes a little practice to get good at the process, but it's worth it.

Flour tortillas

4 cups all-purpose flour

1 tablespoon kosher salt

¾ cup vegetable oil or other cooking fat

2 cups very hot tap water (between 135° and 180°F)

At our restaurant in the Guadalupe Valley, we make tortillas using Central Milling's Artisan Bakers Flour, which is a fancy bread flour preferred by many artisanal bakeries in San Francisco. If you have that kind of flour handy, by all means use it. Specialty bread flours often need less resting to become pliable, and that will help you get great results quickly and easily.

But if you don't have access to specialty flours, don't worry. Throughout Baja, you'll find incredibly delicious tortillas made from whatever inexpensive flour is sold at the local market. The key issue is just to get to know your flour and adjust your process based on how it behaves when you use it in your kitchen.

Besides flour, the other key ingredient of flour tortillas is fat. Many people have a favorite kind of fat to use when making tortillas, whether it's lard, tallow (rendered beef fat), vegetable shortening, or vegetable oil. Each fat has its own flavor subtleties and also will make the tortilla cook a little differently.

When I make tortillas, I use animal fat, just out of respect for the old ways. Tallow would be the most traditional, I think. At Fauna, we use a high-quality lard, because we are getting plenty of it from our farmers.

In any case, use whatever you prefer. You can make delicious tortillas with many different kinds of fat.

The fat and flour types are up to you, but on the following two points I give you no choice. First, for this recipe to really shine, you must use very hot water, using a kettle if necessary to heat it. The recipe works best when the water's temperature is right on the edge of what you can stand. Be careful not to burn yourself with it. And second, you must be willing to spend sufficient time working the dough before forming it. As long as you follow these two guidelines, you can make great tortillas.

Now, if you find yourself having trouble getting the tortillas nice and thin, let the dough rest longer between every step. Your specific flour and water will have its own characteristics, and you don't know until you work with it how pliable it will be. But, in the end, you just have to keep kneading it enough and resting it enough until you get that super-thin quality that makes *norteño* tortillas—flour tortillas from the northern parts of Mexico—distinctive.

If you are having trouble with the dough sticking to your fingers or surfaces at any point in the process, try dusting the dough or your implements with a little flour. You can also experiment with keeping your hands a little wetter, or even lightly oiled with the fat you're using. Trust me, tortilla-making gets a lot easier with repetition. Don't worry if your first tortillas don't come out perfectly. Keep doing it, and they will get great before you know it!

After you make and shape the dough, you're going to need a griddle to cook the tortillas on. Well-seasoned cast iron works great for this, as does any modern nonstick surface in good condition.

It's best to make tortillas shortly before the meal at which you're going to eat them. Handmade tortillas go stale if left for even a few hours at room temperature or in the fridge. However, they do freeze acceptably well, so you can always make a slightly bigger batch than you need and put some in the freezer in case you need one later in a pinch.

Put the flour and salt in a large mixing bowl. Whisk the mixture while you very slowly pour the oil into the bowl. Continue whisking until all the oil is incorporated. This should take only a couple minutes; the flour will remain grainy, but it will assume a darker color and clump up a little bit. A little clumpiness is fine, but try to spread the oil through the mixture as best as you can.

Once you've put all the oil in, work the dough with your hands while adding the hot water little by little. Be careful not to burn

continued

Flour tortillas, continued

yourself with the water. Keep kneading the dough until you have a pliable, homogeneous mass. This could take 2 minutes of work, or 15 minutes. Stop kneading when the dough is smooth and only a little bit sticky. Cover it and let it rest. This relaxes the dough so it will stretch better later. Depending on your flour, the resting period will be between 20 minutes and a couple hours. It's ready when it's a little bit fluffy, not sticky.

Shape the rested dough into balls a little smaller than golf balls or dessert truffles. Roll each one between your hands to compact it. Expect to have about twenty-four dough balls. If you have time, let the balls rest again for up to 1 hour, which will make them a little easier to form. Then place them on a baking sheet to prepare them for shaping. Warm your griddle, well-seasoned cast-iron skillet, or nonstick pan over medium-high heat.

Flour your work surface. Using your hands, a rolling pin, or a tortilla press, shape a dough ball into a tortilla 6 or 8 inches in diameter. Ideally, the tortilla will be so thin that you can partially see through the dough. You may have to press it partway out, dust it with flour, and then finish pressing it, so that it holds its shape better. If you are using a tortilla press, you may want to line it with wax paper or a lightly-oiled cut-up ziplock bag, to make it easier to remove the tortilla after pressing. With a spatula or your hands, move the first tortilla onto your hot griddle. If you used a lined tortilla press, you can flop the tortilla onto your fingertips and then delicately drop it into the pan. Cook the tortilla for 30 to 60 seconds on each side, flipping it when it puffs up. The tortilla should cook up with some golden spots. If it quickly develops dark brown spots, turn down the heat for the pan. When the tortilla is done, put it in a tortilla warmer on the counter, or inside a towel. (We don't usually keep them warm in the oven, as that can make them dry and crumbly.) Repeat the pressing and cooking process with the remaining dough balls. Now you have great homemade tortillas!

Serve as soon as the rest of your meal is ready.

Pork salpicón

Kosher salt

3 tablespoons sugar

1 to 1½ pounds pork jowl
(or belly, rib, or shoulder),
skin removed and excess
fat trimmed

1 bay leaf

3 dried pasilla chiles (also
known as chile negro)

½ medium avocado, or to taste

2 medium tomatillos

1 serrano chile

5 sprigs cilantro

2 tablespoons lime juice

4 teaspoons extra-virgin
olive oil

Much of Latin America has a traditional dish called *salpicón*.
It's a kind of chilled salad of shredded beef tossed with some
produce; in Mexico, the produce usually includes avocado, onions,
chiles, and lime juice. I worked at one restaurant where we made
a seafood *salpicón* with pan-fried fish, which came across a little
like a ceviche except that the crispiness of the fish created a
great combination of textures.

In developing my menu at Fauna, I wanted a dish that captured
that textural mix while also showcasing some unique ingredients
we have in the Guadalupe Valley—specifically the Berkshire
pork being raised by our friend Tito Cortes. And, because it can
get pretty hot here in the summer, we often crave bright, cool-
temperature dishes that feel refreshing to eat. For those reasons,
we put together this pork *salpicón*.

Because it's served at room temperature or even a little cooler,
this pork *salpicón* makes a great appetizer for a summer grill-out
or get-together. The pork holds its crispness in a way that beef
doesn't quite, and the acidity of the dish makes it refreshing like
a *crudo*, even though it's a fully cooked meat dish. I think this is
a very Baja-style take on something that is traditionally a little
heavier.

I like to use pork jowl for this dish because it has a great balance
of fat and lean and it's a very delicious cut. If you have access
to a full-service butcher, they should have jowl available. If not,
you can use belly, rib meat, or even a shoulder, adjusting the
cooking time as needed. If you buy a larger cut of pork, consider
cutting it into 1-inch-thick pieces to keep the cooking time under
a few hours.

Mix 2 tablespoons salt and the sugar with enough water that you end up with sufficient liquid for marinating the pork. The exact ratio of salt-sugar to water isn't very important; as long as you have roughly the given ratio of salt-sugar to meat, it will be great. Marinate the jowl in a bowl or ziplock bag with the salt-sugar liquid for 3 hours.

Preheat the oven to 400°F.

Put the jowl and marinade in a roasting pan, along with the bay leaf and pasillas. Add water to the pan until the jowl is fully covered. Cover the pan with aluminum foil. Bake for 3 hours. The pork should be falling apart at this point. Remove the meat from the water and set it aside. You can discard the other contents of the roasting pan.

Raise the oven temperature to 450°F.

Cut the avocado and tomatillos into small cubes and put them in a mixing bowl. Dice the serrano as small as you can and add it to the bowl. Remove the cilantro leaves from the stems and add the leaves to the bowl, discarding the stems. Add the lime juice and oil to the bowl and stir to mix. Season with salt, then set aside.

Put the jowl on a sheet pan and return it to the oven for 8 minutes or until it crisps. Remove the pork and let it cool until it is at your desired serving temperature.

Mix the pork in with the tomatillo/avocado salad and serve immediately.

Grilled vegetables

1 zucchini

8 green beans

¼ Chayote squash

⅔ cup mushrooms

1 serrano chile

Olive oil for coating

¼ cup soy sauce

¼ cup mirin, dry sherry, off-dry wine, or sweet wine

Juice from 1 lime

This recipe is nice alongside any of the meat-based dishes in this book. It's particularly well-suited for outdoor cooking, but you can also cook this using your broiler or a large frying pan. It might be surprising to see Japanese ingredients such as mirin and soy sauce in a Mexican cookbook. In Baja, we have a lot of influence from all over the Pacific Rim. In fact, our famous fish tacos are (perhaps apocryphally) said to be derived from tempura. And Mexicali, the capital of our state, which welcomed many Chinese immigrants in the early twentieth century, remains known for its Chinese restaurants. Today, with the names of Pacific Rim manufacturers, seafood exporters, and shipping companies emblazoned on containers crisscrossing the peninsula, many Mexican cooks incorporate traditionally Asian ingredients and flavors with increasing ease.

Preheat the grill to medium. Cut the zucchini, green beans, squash, and mushrooms as you wish; I like them a little bigger than bite-size. Put them in a bowl with the serrano and add just enough oil to lightly coat them.

Mix the soy sauce and mirin in a separate bowl. Pour half of the soy-mirin mixture into the bowl with the vegetables and toss the veggies to coat them. Set the rest of the soy-mirin mixture aside. Cook the vegetables (including the mushrooms and chile) on the grill until tender, 5 to 15 minutes. Adjust the heat and the vegetables' position as needed so that, when the vegetables are cooked, their skin blisters without being burnt.

As the vegetables cook, add the lime juice to the remaining soy-mirin mixture.

Remove the vegetables from the grill and put all of them except the serrano in or on your serving plate(s) or bowl(s). Chop the serrano into thin slices and mix the slices in with the rest. Top with the soy-mirin-lime marinade. Serve immediately.

ON BEANS

In making a cookbook of Mexican food—even food from Mexico's California—of course we are going to talk about cooking beans!

You can probably find as many ways to cook beans as there are people who cook them. If you already cook beans, you likely have a preferred method, and I won't try to talk you out of it. Many traditional recipes call for aromatic vegetables such as onions, often some meat, and perhaps a mix of spices. These recipes make delicious beans.

However, I want to suggest another approach to cooking beans, which I use, and which we detail in our Basic Beans (page 51). In this method, we cook a pot of beans with only water and a little bit of salt.

We use this method for two reasons.

The first reason is that beans taste great! And, in cooking with only water and salt, we bring forth their beany-ness as much as possible. This comes in handy later when we add them to a dish (such as Octopus and Domingo Rojo Beans, page 199) as a specific flavor element. Then we get the bean flavor we want, and we can add other flavors separately, in the exact amount and form we want. This makes us more precise, and better, cooks.

The second reason, which is related, is that we almost always make a large pot of beans well beforehand and then cook the beans we are going to serve a second time as part of a separate recipe. That second cooking is a great time to add any additional flavors, if desired, that might improve our specific dish. The second cooking might be making refried beans (for which we add cooking fat and onions) or heating the beans in a pan as part of a burrito filling. We can even add a little fresh-squeezed lime juice before adding them cold to a dish. Keeping the initial cooking as simple as possible helps us present the beans in the way that's best when we actually serve them.

Basic beans

1 pound dried beans

8 cups hot tap water

1 tablespoon kosher salt

This is a basic template that you may have to adjust depending on the type and age of beans you are using. For soft beans that take on a lot of water, you may need to add a little more water than noted here and shorten the cooking time a little. For harder beans, which can include many heirloom beans from Mexico—as well as beans that have been sitting a while in the pantry—you may need a little less water to finish with the right balance of bean liquor to beans, and also you may need to increase the cooking time somewhat.

For more information on where you can buy heirloom beans, see page 252.

Notice that we have not discussed soaking the beans. While I know that in the United States there can be a bit of contention between those who do and those who do not soak beans before cooking, in Mexico, that is not often something we do. This recipe assumes the beans have not been soaked.

Preheat the oven to 250°F.

Wash the beans in a colander, removing any rocks or hollow beans.

Put the beans and water in a Dutch oven or oven-safe pot with lid. Place the covered pot in the oven and bake for 100 minutes. Uncover, add the salt, and stir the beans a little bit with a wooden spoon to help dissolve the salt into the water.

Re-cover and bake for 15 minutes more, or longer if needed to attain the desired texture.

Pull the pot from the oven, remove the lid, and let cool. Transfer the beans to a large jar or bowl along with enough liquor to keep them submerged. You might have quite a bit more bean liquor remaining after that; you can discard it. The beans will keep in the fridge for up to 2 weeks.

In Baja, we are Californians, we are also Mexicans, and we eat tacos pretty often. My hometown of Ensenada is justly famous for fish tacos (see page 130). Fish taco stands usually open in the morning and close in the early evening. If you want something later at night to soak up a few beers, you're probably going to be stopping for tacos made with meat. My favorite type of meat tacos is the kind called *norteño* ("northerner") tacos.

Norteño tacos feature chopped steak meat and toppings in a flour tortilla. Some places add a melty white cheese, like mozzarella. As you might guess from the name, this is the signature style of taco in much of Mexico's far north, not just Baja.

Carne asada, usually the main ingredient of *norteño* tacos, is Spanish for "flame-grilled meat." You can make *carne asada* from any of several cuts of beef, depending on the dish. For tacos, the preferred cut is skirt steak, which is usually called *arrachera*.

The best *arrachera* taco places use very thin steaks cooked over wood coals. After the meat is cooked, your *taquero*—the taco artist serving you—puts the steak on a cutting board made from a tree trunk and dices it with a cleaver, as if you're at Benihana. Then he puts the meat in a tortilla and you get your taco. The experience of watching this preparation, of course, makes the taco taste even better.

If you don't have a wood-fired grill at your disposal, you can make great *arrachera* in a pan or on a griddle. It's technically not *carne asada*, but it's still delicious.

Arrachera in salsa negra

---

1 pound skirt steak (or flank
steak), about ½ inch thick, cut
to a length short enough to fit
in your pan

1 teaspoon kosher salt

2 tablespoons neutral cooking
oil, such as canola oil

For serving

1 cup Salsa Negra (page 56)

Refried beans (see page 32)
and flour tortillas (see page 38)
or a sliced baguette (optional)

You can cook *arrachera* (skirt steak) on a grill over a wood fire,
which makes it a kind of *carne asada*. Or you can use a griddle
or a skillet, which makes the dish technically not *carne asada*
but does make it easier to keep in the juices that give the cut
its distinctive quality. This recipe is for a skillet, but it's easy to
change to cooking over fire if you want to. To do so, just brush
a little oil on the skirt steak before cooking, instead of putting
the oil in the pan—or even skip the oil altogether if you want
a drier crisp on the meat.

Put the meat in a bowl and sprinkle it with the salt. Let it sit
for an hour, either at room temperature or in the fridge.

Warm the oil in a skillet over medium-high heat.

When the pan is hot, add the steak and cook on both sides,
flipping it every minute or so, until it has an internal temperature
of 145°F. (If you don't have an instant-read thermometer, pull
the steak out of the pan when the meat feels like your cheek
when you poke it.) Transfer the meat to a cutting board and let
it rest for 5 minutes.

If you are making tacos, chop the meat first against the grain
and then with the grain to make pieces about ¾-inch square.
Otherwise, serve the steaks on a plate bathed in the salsa
negra, accompanied by refried black beans and flour tortillas
or a sliced baguette, if desired.

Salsa negra
(black sauce)

---

1 cup lard or other cooking oil or fat (more or less depending on the size of your pan)

3 ounces dried chipotle chile

½ cup water, or as needed

4 teaspoons sugar

Kosher salt

This sauce is made from pan-fried chipotle chiles. You can fry the chiles in any kind of cooking fat, but for this recipe, I prefer the flavor of lard. Note that *salsa* just means "sauce" in Spanish, and while some salsas are used as dips, not all salsas are! This salsa, which is pretty hot, is more of the type for spicing up meat than for eating with chips.

Lard has recently acquired a reputation in the United States for being unhealthful, but if you have a source of "clean" lard (made from wholesomely raised pigs, with no chemicals added to the rendered fat), I think it's actually on the healthier side compared to most cooking oils. More important, in terms of cooking, lard is stable up to a reasonably high temperature (its smoke point is 370°F), and its flavor goes well with a lot of other ingredients. See page 253 for sourcing suggestions for dried chipotles.

Heat the lard to 350°F in a deep pan or Dutch oven. The lard should be at least ¼ inch deep when melted. Add the chipotle to the lard and fry until it has a brown color and crunchy texture, 5 to 10 minutes.

Remove the chile and put it in a food processor. Puree, while adding the water to thin the sauce to a liquid. If the sauce stays clumpy, add some of the melted lard to thin it out.

Stir in the sugar and season with salt. Salsa negra will keep in the fridge for up to 1 week.

Norteño tacos

12 flour tortillas (see page 38)

16 ounces mozzarella cheese, shredded

1 pound cooked *arrachera*, diced and hot from the grill (see page 55)

1 cup Salsa Negra (page 56)

1 pint cooked beans (see page 51), reheated

1 white onion, peeled and diced

1 bunch cilantro, chopped

1 cup Tomatillo/Avocado Sauce (page 78)

For serving

1 cup Tangy Red Salsa (page 136)

Norteño tacos are popular all throughout Baja; every town has a favorite place or two. Close to the border, in Rosarito, there is a famous stand called Tacos El Yaqui. They call their taco a *"perrón"*—a made-up word that translates to something like the American slang phrase "the big dog"—and it includes beans and melted cheese along with more conventional fixin's. In some other places, a taco with melted cheese in it is called a "quesotaco." Either way, including cheese in these tacos is a delicious option.

Warm a greased or nonstick griddle or skillet over medium heat. Put a tortilla on the griddle. After a few seconds, flip the tortilla, put a handful of cheese on it, and spread evenly. When the cheese starts to soften, fold the tortilla in half. As the cheese melts, flip the folded tortilla.

When the cheese has melted, pull the tortilla off the grill. Open it up onto a plate so it lies flat, with the cheese side up.

Along the centerfold of the tortilla, place a line of meat, topped with a little salsa negra. Then top that with beans, onion, cilantro, and tomatillo/avocado sauce. Fold the tortilla back into a taco shape. Repeat with the remaining tortillas.

Serve with the red salsa on the side.

Grilled rabbit
with pasilla chile marinade

2 rabbits, boned

Kosher salt (see Note)

¼ cup vegetable oil,
or as needed

1 cup Pasilla Chile Marinade
(page 64)

For serving

Flour tortillas (see page 38)
or a sliced baguette

2 limes cut into wedges

Outdoor cooking is a big part of life in Baja, and in particular we frequently cook small game—such as rabbits and quail—over fire. This recipe for rabbit works on a wood fire (if you can find mesquite or oak, those would be most typical, but any hardwood will work) or on a charcoal or gas grill.

Set your fire to medium heat. You want the flames low enough that they are not touching the meat as it cooks, but you are not looking for barbecue-style low-and-slow smoking. Rabbits can vary in size, and this recipe will work whether they're big or small; you just have to adjust the cooking time as needed. For medium-size rabbits, you can expect the meat will cook in 15 to 30 minutes.

Whenever you're cooking outdoors, an instant-read thermometer is your best friend. To judge doneness, place the probe in the thickest part of the meat. You want to remove the rabbit from the heat once it has reached 145°F and then set it aside for a few minutes. The internal temperature will continue to rise to 150°F or so, at which point it is fully done.

Note: Use 1 teaspoon salt per 1 pound of rabbit when seasoning.

About 1 hour before cooking, salt the rabbits and let them sit uncovered, either in the fridge or at room temperature.

Bring the grill to medium heat. Once it is hot, brush the grill grates with the oil (so the meat will not stick to them).

Set aside ¼ cup of the marinade. Using a brush, apply a coating of the remaining marinade to the entire exterior of the meat.

Place the marinated rabbits on the grill. The flames should not be touching the meat. Cook, flipping the rabbits and reapplying marinade every 5 minutes, until the interior of each rabbit reaches 145°F as measured with an instant-read thermometer. This will take 15 to 30 minutes for medium-size rabbits over medium heat. Once the temperature is reached, set the meat aside (away from the grill) on a cutting board for 5 minutes. During this time, the rabbits will finish cooking internally on their own.

Using a fork, tear open the rabbits at their meatiest parts or pull the meat off entirely. Pour the reserved marinade over the meat. Serve alongside flour tortillas or a sliced baguette, with lime wedges.

Pasilla chile marinade

---

1 tablespoon neutral cooking oil, such as canola oil, or as needed

1 pound tomatoes, stemmed

¼ pound tomatillos, husked and cleaned

2 dried pasilla chiles

1 garlic clove, peeled

½ medium yellow onion, peeled and coarsely chopped

Kosher salt

Use this lightly spicy salsa as a marinade for meat before grilling, and also as a sauce to dress cooked meat before serving.

Warm the oil in a large saucepot over medium heat, making sure there is enough oil to coat the bottom of the pot.

Put the tomatoes, tomatillos, pasillas, garlic, and onion in the pot. The mixture should sizzle a little bit in the oil. Let it cook, uncovered, stirring occasionally, until the chiles become supple, taking up adequate moisture from the tomatoes and tomatillos, about 10 minutes. Add a little water during the cooking if needed to keep anything from drying out. Remove the pot from the heat when all the ingredients are fully cooked and soft all the way through, about 30 minutes.

Let the ingredients cool slightly and then put them in the bowl of a blender or food processor. Blend them to a liquid and season with salt. Pasilla chile marinade will keep in the fridge for up to 5 days.

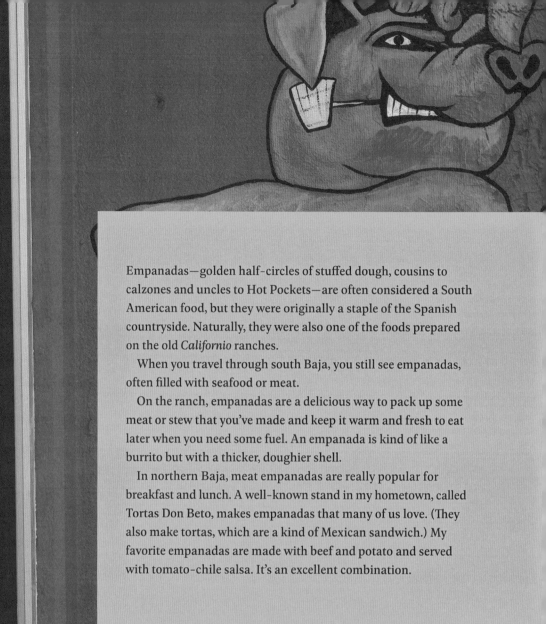

Empanadas—golden half-circles of stuffed dough, cousins to calzones and uncles to Hot Pockets—are often considered a South American food, but they were originally a staple of the Spanish countryside. Naturally, they were also one of the foods prepared on the old *Californio* ranches.

When you travel through south Baja, you still see empanadas, often filled with seafood or meat.

On the ranch, empanadas are a delicious way to pack up some meat or stew that you've made and keep it warm and fresh to eat later when you need some fuel. An empanada is kind of like a burrito but with a thicker, doughier shell.

In northern Baja, meat empanadas are really popular for breakfast and lunch. A well-known stand in my hometown, called Tortas Don Beto, makes empanadas that many of us love. (They also make tortas, which are a kind of Mexican sandwich.) My favorite empanadas are made with beef and potato and served with tomato-chile salsa. It's an excellent combination.

Potato empanadas
with ground beef

1 small potato (about 4 ounces)

1 teaspoon neutral cooking oil, such as canola oil

⅓ cup white onion, peeled and diced

Kosher salt

4 ounces ground beef

½ cup Tomato Sauce for Meat (page 71)

1 pound flour tortilla dough (see page 38), up through resting

Deep-frying fat as needed

This empanada recipe uses the same dough as the flour tortilla recipe found at the beginning of this book. To moisten the filling, the recipe also uses some of the same tomato sauce that is served alongside the empanadas.

You'll need a deep pot for frying the empanadas. Because empanadas are pretty small, usually a deep saucepan will work. Attach a candy thermometer to the side to ensure the oil stays at the correct temperature. Also it's good to use a grease screen over the saucepan to keep hot oil from splattering. See "On Deep-Frying at Home" (page 128) for more detailed instruction.

Dice the potato into cubes about ¼ inch per side. Set aside.

Warm the cooking oil in a pan over medium heat. Add the potato and cook for 5 minutes. Add the onion to the pan. Season with ¼ teaspoon salt and cook for 5 minutes more.

Add the ground beef and ¼ teaspoon salt to the pan and cook, stirring, for 3 minutes. Pour the tomato sauce into the mixture and cover the pan until the potatoes and meat are fully cooked, about 20 minutes. Set this mixture aside.

On a flat surface, spread out the flour tortilla dough. Tear off pieces that will make a ball that fits neatly in your hand.

With a rolling pin, flatten each dough ball until it is a little more than 3 inches in diameter. It should be about ¼ inch thick.

Bring your frying fat to 350°F, measured using a candy/frying thermometer. You need about 3 inches of fat to cover the empanada during frying.

continued

Potato empanadas, continued

Put some of the meat-potato mixture onto the center of the dough, using a large spoon (draining any excess liquid back into the pan). The filling should cover the whole disc of dough except for about ¼ inch on the edges.

Fold the dough in half, and then pinch the edges down so that the filling is totally sealed. You want it sealed enough so, during the next step (frying), no filling comes out of the empanada and no oil goes in. Repeat with each dough ball and the remaining filling. (You can also start frying the first empanada and then form the remainder of empanadas.)

Line a plate with paper towels.

Add each empanada to the hot oil and fry until it has a golden-colored crust and slightly crunchy texture, 4 to 6 minutes. As you remove each empanada from the pot, place it on the paper towel–lined plate to wick away any extra oil and then sprinkle with salt.

Enjoy the empanadas right away or set aside to serve as canapés. They will keep well at room temperature for up to 3 hours.

Tomato sauce for meat

---

3 red tomatoes, stemmed

1½ yellow onions, peeled

2 teaspoons neutral cooking oil, such as canola oil

2 garlic cloves, peeled

2 serrano chiles

1 ounce dried guajillo chiles, stemmed

Kosher salt

Meat or fish in a sauce, served alongside flour tortillas and fixin's such as beans, salsa, chiles, onions, and cilantro is an everyday type of meal in Baja. This recipe is for a tomato-chile sauce that goes well with many meats. It's used in Potato Empanadas with Ground Beef (page 68), and I also use it as a serving sauce for shredded beef, pulled pork, or braised lamb.

Cut the tomatoes and onion into eighths.

Cover the bottom of a saucepan with the oil and put it over medium-low heat.

Add the tomatoes to the pan. When they have softened (typically after 2 to 3 minutes), add the onions. Cook for about 3 minutes, until onions start to glisten, adding water if necessary so that they don't burn. Then add the garlic and continue to stir and add water as needed to avoid burning anything. When the garlic cloves have softened slightly (again after 2 to 3 minutes), add the serranos.

Keep cooking the mixture, stirring regularly and adding small amounts of water, if needed, until the tomatoes are very fragile and the other ingredients crush easily under a wooden spoon. This should be about 10 minutes more. Remove from the heat and set aside.

In a separate saucepan, bring 3 inches of water to boil. Lower the heat to a simmer and add the guajillos, cooking and rehydrating, for 15 minutes. They should be fully rehydrated at this point. Remove the chiles from the pot but don't pour out the water.

Put the guajillos and the tomato mixture in the bowl of a blender or food processor. Puree everything into a smooth, silky texture. During the process, add the guajillo water as needed to liquefy the mixture.

Last, season with salt and blend for a couple more pulses. The sauce will keep in the fridge for up to 1 week.

Honey-roasted duck

2 ducks (4 to 5 pounds each), skin left on, cleaned and dressed

½ cup butter

5 teaspoons kosher salt

¼ cup honey, warmed to liquid state

This simple recipe for roasted duck can be used as the base for several other recipes, including Duck Sopes (page 75), Duck in Demi-Glace with Eggplant Puree (page 204), and Duck Tamal in Black Chipotle Sauce (page 207). To get the best flavor from ducks, you need to dry-age them, which is easy to do in your fridge. I recommend letting the ducks age for 1 week, sitting unpackaged on a wire rack above a flat pan.

To make the glaze for the duck skin, you'll need honey that has been warmed to the point of being a fairly thin liquid. The challenge is that temperatures above 110°F can change the character of honey. So, when you're heating honey in its jar, keep the temperature below 110°F but still warm enough to liquefy the honey.

The most reliable way to warm the honey without cooking it is to put the jar in a water bath with the temperature closely monitored to be at or below 110°F. If you have a circulator (sous vide machine) at home, it's perfect for the task. If not, I recommend using a Dutch oven or large bowl full of hot water sitting on the counter, with the water temperature measured with an instant-read thermometer, and the bowl periodically touched up with hot water from a kettle to maintain adequate heat.

Note: As the glaze cooks and as the fat drips from the birds, a certain amount of smoke may be generated. That's okay. But be sure to keep your cooking area well ventilated so the smoke dissipates.

Place the ducks on a wire rack over a flat pan. Leave the ducks on the wire rack with the cavity facing down to facilitate their blood draining out onto the pan over time. Place the ducks in your fridge, uncovered, and leave to age for 7 days.

When you're ready to cook the ducks, pull them out of the fridge at least 1 hour—ideally 2 to 3 hours—before cooking so they have time to fully reach room temperature. Preheat the oven to 450°F.

continued

Honey-roasted duck, continued

In a frying pan over low heat, slowly brown the butter and then season with 1 teaspoon of the salt.

Put the brown butter in a small mixing bowl and then slowly add the liquefied honey, stirring constantly. Using a brush, fully bathe the ducks on both sides with this glaze. Then salt the ducks with the remaining 4 teaspoons salt.

Put the ducks on a rack in a roasting pan, breast-side up. Bake the ducks until their deepest internal temperature is 135°F as measured by an instant-read thermometer. Depending on the size of the ducks and their starting temperature, the cooking will take between 15 and 45 minutes.

Remove the ducks from the oven and let them rest another 15 minutes. During this time, the internal temperature of the ducks will reach 140°F. (Here we note, without comment, that the USDA recommends cooking duck to a much higher internal temperature, 170°F.)

Once the duck has cooled slightly, pull the meat from the carcass. If you're planning to make a stock or demi-glace, save the carcass. You can freeze both the pulled meat and carcass if you're not going to use them right away. For best quality, use all parts of the duck within 1 month of freezing.

Duck sopes

High-temperature cooking oil, such as canola oil or avocado oil, as needed

6 ounces corn masa
(see page 142)

Kosher salt

2 ounces refried beans
(see page 32)

2 ounces Honey-Roasted Duck
(page 72)

2 to 3 big leaves of lettuce, chopped

Mexican crema or sour cream for dolloping

For serving

Tomatillo/Avocado Sauce
(page 78)

Sopes of various kinds are a staple throughout Mexican cooking. They are, like tostadas, a preparation of masa (nixtamalized corn) that is typically covered with delicious toppings. The difference between sopes and tostadas is that, with sopes, the masa discs are generally thicker, with a slightly crisped outside and a fluffy interior.

This recipe calls for topping the sopes with pulled duck—a favorite ingredient in restaurants of north Baja—and a traditional Mexican salsa verde. You can also make sopes with any other meat or meat/sauce combination that suits you. The dish even works well by replacing (or topping) the meat with a poached egg for a Mexican-Californian brunch treat.

Cover the bottom of a frying pan (well-seasoned cast iron works great for this) with a generous amount of cooking oil, and warm it over medium heat.

Divide the masa into four equal balls. They should be a little smaller than golf balls. Using your hands, shape them into patties about ½ inch thick. Then use your thumbs to make small divots in the center of both sides of each patty. At this point they should look something like fat, circular earlobes with a depression in the center on both sides. This is your starting place for shaping the sopes.

Working from the center divot to the edge of each patty, gently press out each sope, aiming for a final disc that is thinner than a smartphone but thicker than a tortilla. Expect it to be about the diameter of a coaster. If you are feeling like an expert sope shaper, you can add a tiny lip around the edge, which will help keep the toppings from sliding off at serving time.

Line a plate with paper towels. Turn the frying pan heat to high, waiting a minute or two for the oil on the bottom of the pan to heat up. Place each masa disc in the pan (as many discs as will

continued

Duck sopes, continued

fit comfortably). Lightly salt the exposed side of each disc and cook them for about 45 seconds. Then flip them, lightly salt the other side, and cook for another 45 seconds.

At this point, let the sopes cook in the pan until they are a rich golden brown, about 5 minutes more, flipping as necessary with a spatula. You may see some small dark brown spots where the highest points of the sopes are burning slightly in contact with the pan. This is okay, and it adds a little complexity to the flavor.

When the sopes are fully cooked, they will be somewhat rigid and easy to handle with the spatula, but they should not be hard like crackers. At this point, remove the sopes from the pan and place them on the paper towel–lined plate to wick away any excess oil, flipping them once on the paper towel if both sides show oil.

Top each disc with an equal share of the refried beans and then place the duck meat on top of the beans. Finish each one with lettuce and a dollop of Mexican crema.

Serve the sopes alongside a bowl of tomatillo/avocado sauce, which each sope-eater can spoon over their meal, bite by bite, to their heart's content.

Tomatillo/avocado sauce

½ pound tomatillos, cleaned, with husks and stems removed

½ small bunch cilantro, thick part of the stems removed

2 garlic cloves, peeled

2 avocados

Juice from 1 lime

Up to 1 serrano chile, stemmed (optional)

½ cup water, or as needed

½ teaspoon kosher salt

This is a *salsa verde* ("green sauce") made with avocado, in the style of the sauces you often see set out at taco stands and other casual eateries. Usually you apply it to your food yourself, choosing how much you want based on your preferences and the spiciness of the sauce. If you use a whole serrano chile when making this recipe, the sauce will be pretty hot! If you don't add much serrano, or if you skip it entirely, the sauce will be mild enough that you can also spread it on a sandwich or even eat it as a dip.

Using a blender or food processor, blend the tomatillos, cilantro, garlic, avocados, lime juice, serrano chile (if using), and water until smooth. While blending, add a little more water if needed to achieve a smoother consistency.

Add the salt, blend a couple pulses more, and serve.

ON MEXICAN CREMA, SOUR CREAM, AND CRÈME FRAÎCHE

Many of our recipes call for "Mexican crema." In Mexico, we often use this ingredient in places where U.S. cooks might use sour cream, and sometimes also where they might use heavy cream. Usually, sour cream is listed as a substitute for Mexican crema, but flavorwise, French crème fraîche is probably closer. Mexican crema is quite a bit less tangy than sour cream, and also a bit sweet. Mexican crema tends to be a little thinner, as well.

You can find Mexican crema at Latino supermarkets, small Mexican grocery stores, and in the Mexican or "international" section of large mainstream supermarkets. Also, in a lot of places, your average minimart is likely to have it as well. El Mexicano and Cacique are two widely available brands.

If you need to make your own substitute for crema, the standard American practice is to mix heavy cream and buttermilk in equal parts. That said, you can also just use sour cream or crème fraîche. It won't taste precisely authentic, but it will probably taste good. And that's most important, after all!

2

FROM THE SEA

To eat in Baja is to enjoy seafood, particularly shellfish and crustaceans. While the Andalusian-influenced food of the Spanish *ranchos* is still a signature of our culture, long before the Spanish were here, the people of Baja lived off the largesse of the sea.

In many towns, even today, you can sit at a beachside stand eating fresh ceviche and watching men use their hands to pull octopuses from the tidal rocks and put them into five-gallon buckets. Down the street from where I live, there's a dockside restaurant where I like to eat extremely fresh oysters while the fishermen in their *pangas*—flat-bottomed fishing boats—return with their catch, from miles out in the Pacific. The rhythm of the ocean harvest is, often, the beat of our daily life.

Note: *After the mussels recipe on page 88, we present these seafood dishes in the order you might serve them at a party. We begin with light, acid-forward plates and then move to fuller-bodied preparations, culminating in the signature festival stew of Old Baja.*

From the house I grew up in, it's about a fifty-meter walk to the ocean. You won't see a lot of trees or anything along the shore, just some scrubby plants and a dirt path along the water where people walk and jog. The first time I ate sea urchin, my dad showed me how to find them among the tidal rocks there and then break them open and scoop out the edible "tongue." Other times, we pulled mussels off the same rocks, and octopuses, too.

Sixty years earlier, my mom's father had set up lobster traps here and harvested Pacific spiny lobsters, which he sold into Texas and other parts of the United States. Later, her brother's tuna fleet operated from the harbor just to the north, near where there's still a good spot for catching flounder from the shore if you know where to cast.

Our house didn't have a lot of electronic entertainment when I was a child, and I didn't have any brothers or sisters, so I ran around pretty freely and attached myself to whoever was there. Sometimes friends would come over, and we would play basketball or soccer. Other times I just hung out and socialized with the crabs on the beach. I remember there was one group of guys, beach guys, who would harvest mussels and then start a bonfire and steam them right there on the shore. My mom would never let me join them, though; to this day I still don't know why. But I would say that's some pretty classic Baja cooking.

Mussels "playitas"
with chorizo

4 cups water

3 ounces dried guajillo chiles, stemmed

1 onion, peeled

4 garlic cloves, peeled

5 whole cloves

5 bay leaves

2 teaspoons black pepper

35 almonds

¼ cup red wine vinegar

1 pound ground pork

1½ teaspoons kosher salt

1 tablespoon neutral cooking oil, such as canola oil

⅞ cup butter

24 mussels

Juice of 1 lemon

½ bunch cilantro, leaves only (optional)

This mix of mussels and pork is how we might serve a group of friends at our place at the little stretch of shore called Playitas. When I was a kid, and my family planned a festive meal, we'd often start by pulling the shellfish off the rocks ourselves. Anyway, it works equally well to buy mussels, as long as you have a good market selling them. Just make sure they're fresh. And, if any mussels don't open on their own when they're cooked, throw those ones out.

Preheat the oven to 350°F.

In a medium pot, bring the water to a rolling boil. Add the guajillos, onion, garlic, cloves, bay leaves, and black pepper. Boil for 10 minutes. Using a strainer to catch and return any stray ingredients, pour out the water, and set the pot aside.

Lay the almonds out in a small tray and put them in the oven for 4 minutes to toast. Remove them. When they have cooled enough to touch, chop them roughly and set them aside.

Put the chile mixture and red wine vinegar in a blender and puree until the ingredients can't get any smoother. Drain the mixture through a fine sieve into a large bowl. Add the ground pork, toasted almonds, and salt. Using your hands, mix the ingredients in the bowl until they are fully integrated. Then put the bowl in the fridge for 30 minutes.

After the meat has rested, warm the cooking oil in a large pan over medium heat. Add the pork mixture to the pan, stirring lightly to keep it cooking evenly. Cook until the edges of the pork clumps are crispy, about 10 minutes. Then turn off the burner and put a lid on the pan to retain the contents' heat and moisture.

continued

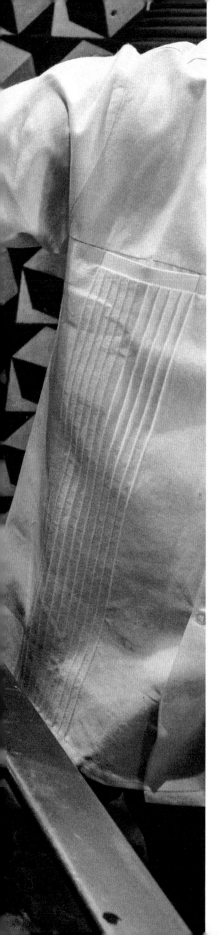

Mussels "playitas," continued

Melt the butter in a large pan over medium heat. Add the mussels and slowly cook them until each mussel is open, about 15 minutes. (If any refuse to open, discard them. Non-opening mussels are those that have gone bad.) Once all the mussels are open, pour the lemon juice over the whole pan, drizzling it over both the mussels and the melted butter.

Remove the pan from the heat. Take the mussels out of the pan and arrange them on a large, deep serving plate. Pour the warm butter over and around the mussels on the plate. Fill each mussel with 1 tablespoon of the cooked meat.

Sprinkle everything with the cilantro, if desired, and serve immediately.

Chocolate clam ceviche

24 pieces uncooked chocolate clam (see "On Cleaning Chocolate Clams," page 94)

1 white onion, peeled and finely diced

1 bunch cilantro, leaves only, finely chopped

1 large tomato, stemmed and diced small

1 cup fresh-squeezed lime juice

3 tablespoons soy sauce

½ cup tomato juice

Kosher salt

1 avocado, sliced (optional)

For serving

Tostaditas (see page 101)

Charred Green Salsa (page 31) and/or Tangy Red Salsa (page 136)

continued

Ceviche—seafood that is "cooked" in citrus juice rather than using heat—is a dish you'll find, in different forms, throughout Latin America. In Baja, we often enjoy ceviche made from our local shellfish.

For many Mexican chefs, ceviche is also an opportunity to get creative with unusual ingredients and flavor combinations. That contrasts with the recipe we give you here, which is a mostly straightforward preparation that you might find anywhere in Baja. I encourage you to use it as a jumping-off point for more elaborate ideas you may come up with.

The main goal of this particular recipe is to fully experience one of the special ingredients of Baja—*almeja chocolata*, or "chocolate clam." This is not a clam made of chocolate. Instead, it gets its name from the distinctive dark brown color of its shell. This clam is often harvested pretty big (sometimes as large as five inches across), and its supple, flavorful meat is very well suited for ceviche. If you can get your hands on some of these clams (see page 253), you will have a particularly authentic Baja feast! If not, you can substitute a different type of clam, or shrimp, or an appropriate sashimi-worthy fish such as albacore tuna or *jurel* (yellowtail jack). Whatever seafood you use, just remove any heads, skin, veins, shells, and/or bones and cut the meat into small pieces before integrating it into the ceviche—as is done here with the clams.

Chocolate clam ceviche, continued

When you are finished shelling and cleaning the clams, chop up the yielded raw clam meat, aiming for pieces about ⅓ inch square. Put the clam meat in a large bowl with the onion, cilantro, and tomato. Add the lime juice and toss all the ingredients in the bowl. Add the soy sauce and tomato juice and toss a little more. Season with salt and let marinate for 5 minutes.

Top the bowl with the avocado slices, if desired. Serve the ceviche alongside tostaditas, with bowl of green salsa and/or red salsa.

On cleaning chocolate clams

To clean the clams, open them carefully with a long knife. Remove and discard any loose goop and place the internal meat mass on your cutting board, setting aside the shell.

The inside of the chocolate clam has three connected parts. The primary portion of clam meat is the fleshy lobe, which is, in part, dark orange. Attached to that lobe is a central complex of hard and soft bits that compose the digestive tract; the backside of that complex includes some edible meat. Last, surrounding the central area is a ring that looks a little like an earlobe and is only lightly connected to the center.

To get the meat for the ceviche, first cut off the lobe with the orange part. That's your first yield of good stuff. Then, using the tip of your knife, detach the earlobe part from the central disc. The earlobe is your second yield. Finally, slice the digestive tract off from its soft backing. The backing is your third bit of yield. (You can throw away the digestive tract or use it to make stock.) Repeat the process with each clam.

Shrimp aguachile

10 dried *chiltepín* chiles or more or less to desired level of heat

Pinch of sugar

Pinch of kosher salt

¼ red onion, peeled

¼ cucumber

Juice from 3 limes (or as needed)

½ pound large shrimp, deveined, shells and heads removed

Pinch of fancy sea salt such as Maldon flakes (or use kosher salt)

In northwest Mexican food, we have another dish that is similar to ceviche. *Aguachile* is a preparation of seafood "cooked" in lime juice and chiles, often incorporating cucumber. The word *aguachile* means "chile water," and the distinguishing characteristic of *aguachile* is that the marinating acid also has some spicy heat. This recipe calls for dried *chiltepín*, a wild chile native to the United States that is sometimes also called "bird's eye" chile. If you can't find it, you can substitute any other source of heat such as dried arbol chiles, fresh habaneros, or even cayenne pepper.

In restaurants or beachside stands, *aguachile* is typically made to order and served immediately. You'll often see diners let it sit for a while before eating. This is to let the shrimp "cook" in the lime juice. In this recipe, we include the time for the shrimp to marinate prior to serving, but you can also serve the dish and let it sit on the table while you chat over a beer with your friends.

Put the *chiltepín* chiles into a blender or food processor with the sugar and salt. Blend them into a powder and set aside.

Slice the red onion as finely as you can. Slice the cucumber into wafer-thin discs. Put the lime juice in a measuring cup or large glass. Add the pepper–salt–sugar powder and stir with a fork.

Halve each shrimp lengthwise and arrange all the shrimp halves in one layer on a plate. Stir the lime juice mixture so that the powder in it is suspended as much as possible and pour the juice all over the shrimp so that each shrimp gets some. (If you don't have enough juice to cover all the shrimp, just squeeze another lime directly over any parts you missed.) Lay the cucumber slices over the shrimp. Top the whole dish with the red onion and finish with the sea salt.

Let the shrimp marinate for 10 to 15 minutes and then serve.

Black aguachile

½ yellow onion, peeled

6 blue corn tortillas
(see page 142, or Purchasing
Notes, page 251)

1 black radish (substitute
another kind of radish
if black radish not available)

¾ cup fresh-squeezed
lime juice, plus 1 or 2 limes
if needed

2⅔ tablespoons extra-virgin
olive oil

2 tablespoons fish sauce

8 grams squid ink or
cuttlefish ink

1 small poblano chile,
stemmed and seeded

¼ teaspoon kosher salt

½ small red onion, peeled

½ pound scallops
(sea scallops or larger)

Aguachile requires citrus juice to "cook" the seafood, and chiles for heat—but all the other details are up to whoever prepares the dish. Throughout Baja, creative aguachiles abound; from neighborhood street carts to high-end restaurants, you will find myriad combinations of seafood and vegetables. The photograph opposite features scallops topped with green cucumber, red radish slices, raw onion rings, and edible flowers.

Once, in a cantina overlooking the Sea of Cortez, I was served an *aguachile* that had been made black by the addition of Maggi sauce (the Mexican version of Worcestershire sauce). It was fun, irreverent, and tangy; when I finished it, I found myself anticipating a world full of even more weird and delightful *aguachiles*. That feeling inspired this recipe, which incorporates squid ink, black radishes, and blue corn tostadas to layer both earthy flavors and shades of gray.

Preheat the oven to 350°F.

Slice the yellow onion as thin as you can; don't worry if the slices break apart. Place the slices and strips in a single layer on a dry sheet pan. Put the pan in the oven and bake for 45 minutes, until the onion pieces are completely dry and burnt to a very dark brown or black. Remove from the oven and scrape the onion off using a spatula. Put the charred onion into a blender or food processor and blend it into a powder. Put the powder in a bowl and set aside. Leave the oven on.

Slice the tortillas into quarters and put them on a baking sheet. Set aside.

Remove the top and bottom tips from the radish and then slice it lengthwise. Using a mandolin or knife, slice the radish into half moon–shaped slices as thin as possible. Then, bisect the half-moons with your knife to make triangular-shaped wafers. Put the wafers in a bowl of ice water and set aside.

continued

In the bowl of a blender or food processor, combine the lime juice, olive oil, fish sauce, squid ink, poblano chile, and salt. Blend until as smooth as possible. Strain through a fine-mesh sieve and put in the fridge.

Cut the red onion the same way you cut the radish, but leave the slices out at room temperature (and don't put them in water).

Slice the scallops into discs, aiming for ⅛-inch-thick slices if you can safely cut them that thin.

In the center of a deep and wide serving dish, arrange the scallop slices in a layer. Surround them with the radish slices and red onion slices. Pour the lime juice mixture over the slices, starting with the scallops and moving outward to the radishes and onions. Make sure that the scallops are fully covered in liquid. If for some reason you can't cover all the scallop pieces in lime juice, grab another lime and squeeze its juice directly over any scallops that got missed. The important thing is that the scallops bathe in the lime juice.

Put the whole dish with the scallops into the fridge. Put the tortilla triangles in the oven until the tortillas are crisp, 15 to 20 minutes.

Remove the scallops from the fridge and sprinkle the burnt onion powder on top of the scallops, onions, and radish. Encircle the aguachile with the baked blue tortilla quarters. Serve immediately.

ON TOSTADITAS

Tostada can be a confusing term in Mexican cuisine because it has multiple meanings. The word *tostada* itself means "toasted." But when used as a noun at the table, the word can mean either a crispy tortilla with various toppings; or it can mean just the crispy tortilla itself. You have to figure out which is being meant just by the context!

Both kinds of tostadas are particularly important to Baja cuisine, where, in addition to tostadas piled with seafood, we also eat a lot of ceviches, *aguachile*, sashimi, and other *crudo* seafood. These "raw bar" dishes are traditionally served with a side of tostadas, much as old-style seafood shacks in the United States accompany their food with oyster crackers or Saltines.

Making things more confusing, the tostadas served alongside seafood are often not actually fried tortillas, they are usually tortilla-shaped corn chips. Often, like restaurant-table Saltines, these tortilla-shaped corn chips are fairly small, so they are sometimes called by the diminutive *tostaditas* ("little tostadas"). Accordingly, in this book we refer to crispy tortillas served alongside a dish as *tostaditas*, and the food item of toppings on a crispy tortilla as a tostada. It doesn't necessarily mean that the tortillas are different sizes, nor does it mean that those are the received distinctions of the words in Mexican Spanish; it's just convenient for our purposes here.

Last, to make tostadas—or *tostaditas*—at home, the easiest thing to do is to bake corn tortillas on a dry baking sheet at 350°F until they are crispy. Alternatively, you can make them in a deep fryer, which gives delicious results and won't take long once your oil is hot. See "On Deep-Frying at Home" (page 128) for frying methods and tips.

Almejas rellenas
(loreto-style stuffed clams)

½ red onion, peeled

1 poblano chile or bell pepper, with stem, pith, and ribs removed

1 garlic clove, peeled and minced

¼ pound bacon

½ pound easily melted cheese, such as *queso asadero* or mozzarella, grated

6 chocolate clams, or other large clam such as cherrystones or chowder clams (about 1½ pounds total)

Almejas rellenas is a specialty of Loreto—a stunning village beside the Sea of Cortez—that showcases the local bounty of chocolate clams. While chocolate clams are traditional for this dish, the recipe also works with any large clam, or, for that matter, other sauté-friendly bivalves of your choice.

You can cook the clams either in the oven or outdoors over fire. If you choose to cook them over mesquite charcoal or hardwood such as oak, you'll get a nice smoke flavor added as well.

Cooking time might vary quite a bit based on the size of your clams and, if you're cooking outdoors, the temperature of your grill. Rather than depend on the cooking times given here, you can instead peel back the foil on a clam—being careful not to burn your fingers—and peek inside to make sure the cheese is melted and everything looks properly cooked.

It's typical to have *tostaditas* (see page 101) and lime wedges on the table, but no accompaniments are really necessary. Honestly, the table isn't necessary either!

Fire up the grill or preheat the oven to 450°F.

Finely dice the onion and poblano chile and put them in a large bowl. Add the minced garlic. Cut the bacon into pieces about ¼ inch on a side and add to the bowl, along with half the cheese. Mix the contents of the bowl thoroughly and set in the fridge.

Open the clams, keeping the hinge intact, and separate the useable meat from the digestive tract as described on page 94. Discard the digestive tracts or save them for making stock. But don't discard the shells; you will need them for cooking. Clean them with water, keeping the shell tops hinged to their bottoms, and set them aside for a moment.

Cut the clam meat into pieces ½ inch on a side or smaller. Then put an equal amount of the clam meat into the bottom of each clamshell. Top with a spoonful of the bacon mixture, making sure the toppings are evenly distributed among each clamshell. Finish each clamshell with the remainder of the grated cheese.

Close all the clamshells and wrap each individual shell completely with aluminum foil. Grill them for 20 minutes or bake in the oven for 12 to 15 minutes.

Pile the foil-wrapped clams on a single plate and serve family-style, letting each guest take a clam, peel the foil back, and get at the deliciousness inside.

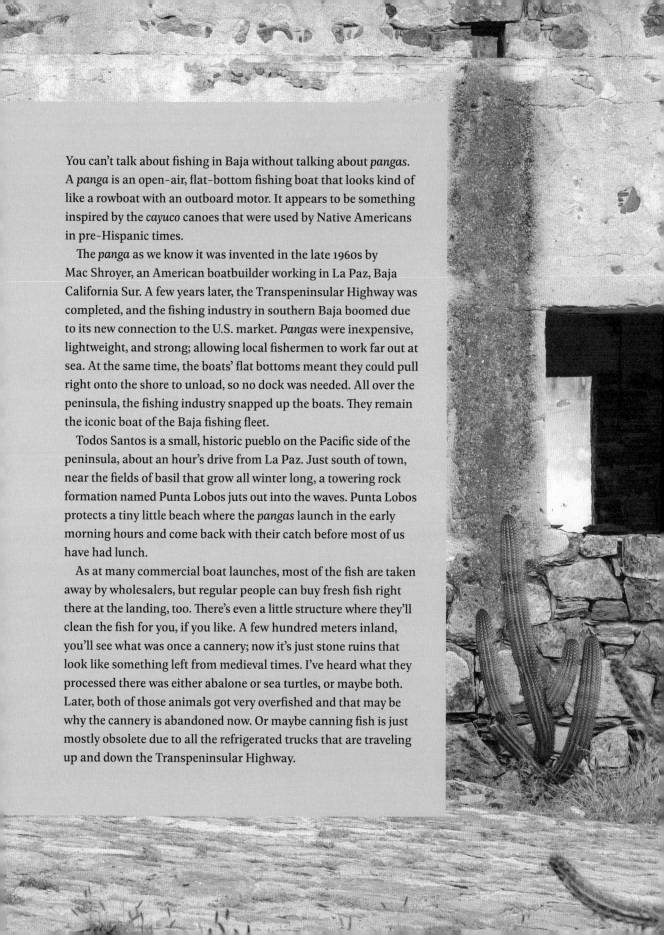

You can't talk about fishing in Baja without talking about *pangas*. A *panga* is an open-air, flat-bottom fishing boat that looks kind of like a rowboat with an outboard motor. It appears to be something inspired by the *cayuco* canoes that were used by Native Americans in pre-Hispanic times.

The *panga* as we know it was invented in the late 1960s by Mac Shroyer, an American boatbuilder working in La Paz, Baja California Sur. A few years later, the Transpeninsular Highway was completed, and the fishing industry in southern Baja boomed due to its new connection to the U.S. market. *Pangas* were inexpensive, lightweight, and strong; allowing local fishermen to work far out at sea. At the same time, the boats' flat bottoms meant they could pull right onto the shore to unload, so no dock was needed. All over the peninsula, the fishing industry snapped up the boats. They remain the iconic boat of the Baja fishing fleet.

Todos Santos is a small, historic pueblo on the Pacific side of the peninsula, about an hour's drive from La Paz. Just south of town, near the fields of basil that grow all winter long, a towering rock formation named Punta Lobos juts out into the waves. Punta Lobos protects a tiny little beach where the *pangas* launch in the early morning hours and come back with their catch before most of us have had lunch.

As at many commercial boat launches, most of the fish are taken away by wholesalers, but regular people can buy fresh fish right there at the landing, too. There's even a little structure where they'll clean the fish for you, if you like. A few hundred meters inland, you'll see what was once a cannery; now it's just stone ruins that look like something left from medieval times. I've heard what they processed there was either abalone or sea turtles, or maybe both. Later, both of those animals got very overfished and that may be why the cannery is abandoned now. Or maybe canning fish is just mostly obsolete due to all the refrigerated trucks that are traveling up and down the Transpeninsular Highway.

Grilled halibut burritos

8 ounces halibut fillet

3 teaspoons olive oil

2 teaspoons kosher salt

1 onion, peeled and diced small

2 poblano chiles or bell peppers, stemmed and diced small

1 teaspoon black pepper

8 flour tortillas (see page 38), warmed

1 lime, cut into quarters

Tomatillo/Avocado Sauce (page 78) for dabbing

Fishermen make this dish in the style of machaca, using whatever fresh catch is on hand instead of beef. Before refrigeration was widespread in Baja's fishing villages, the fish for this recipe might have been smoked and dried for storage and then rehydrated in a pan before eating. That's not necessary now, but you can still use that rehydration technique with leftover fish that may have dried out a little over a couple days. I know a fisherman/chef who intentionally leaves his cooked fish uncovered in the fridge before making this dish, to help it dry out and develop a more intense flavor.

Our recipe calls for the fish to be cooked on an outdoor grill. If you don't have access to a grill, you can cook it on a sheet pan in your oven, browning the outside first in the broiler and then putting the fillet in the oven at 400°F.

Heat your grill to its maximum temperature.

Brush both sides of the halibut with 1 teaspoon of the olive oil. Salt the fish with 1 teaspoon of the salt.

Put the fish on the preheated grill for about 30 seconds on each side and then turn the temperature on the grill to medium. Cook for about 10 minutes (depending on the thickness of the fish), flipping once, until the internal temperature of the fillet is 130°F as measured with an instant-read thermometer. Remove the fish to a plate or cutting board and let rest for 20 minutes. Then shred or crumble the fish into small pieces, using a knife if needed. (You can make the halibut into machaca at this time, or you can store the fish for up to several days in the fridge, uncovered, to encourage it to dry out a little bit.)

In a frying pan over medium heat, put the remaining 2 teaspoons olive oil followed immediately by the onion. Stir occasionally and add a little water as needed so the onion doesn't burn. Once the onion pieces have started to soften (about 5 minutes), add the chiles. Cook and stir until the chiles have softened, about 5 minutes. Again, add water as needed to keep the onion and chiles from dehydrating, burning, or sticking to the pan. Add the black pepper and remaining 1 teaspoon salt.

By now the onion should have released its moisture, and you can expect to have a thin layer of liquid at the bottom of the pan. If not, add a little water. Turn the heat to high and then add the halibut, stirring constantly to ensure that the fish is heated evenly and absorbs some water. Remove the fish once it is heated, which will take 2 to 3 minutes.

Using a serving spoon, scoop an equal amount of the fish mixture into each tortilla and serve them open face, with a lime wedge. Before eating, squeeze the lime onto the fish, dab on some tomatillo/avocado sauce, and roll the tortilla into a cylinder around it, into a Mexican-style burrito.

Oysters on the half shell
with chicharrones and mignonette

Juice of 3 limes

1 tablespoon finely
minced shallot

¼ teaspoon ground
black pepper

½ cup chicharrones
(see page 114)

12 oysters

1 sprig cilantro, finely
minced (optional)

Fresh oysters on the half shell are a joy of living near the Pacific Ocean. Baja is perhaps best known for its big and briny Bahia Falsa oysters, but we also raise small, sweet Kumamotos and many other varieties. Like people everywhere in North America, we like oysters with a squeeze of citrus and some hot sauce, or even just plain from the shell. A classic mignonette, as used in this recipe, is always a favorite, with limes–ubiquitous in the Mexican pantry–substituting for vinegar. And *chicharrón* crumbles make a perfect topping, evoking both the bacon and bread crumbs of oysters Rockefeller, without having to cook the oyster meat itself.

If you find yourself driving back from the beach with an ice chest full of fresh oysters, and you don't have the ingredients for this recipe handy, you can stop at a gas station and get fried pork rinds and limes. Skip the pepper, shallot, and cilantro, and just top the oysters with fresh-squeezed lime and crushed *chicharrones*. That's close enough to call it Baja cooking.

Use a fork to stir together the lime juice, shallot, and pepper in a bowl or measuring cup. Let this mignonette sit for at least 15 minutes and as long as 2 hours. Pour the sauce into a small serving bowl or ramekin.

Crush the *chicharrones* into a coarse powder using a masher or a *metate*. If you don't have a good crushing tool, just put the *chicharrones* in a bag, fold the top over so they don't fly out, lay the bag on the counter, and go to town on it.

Shuck the oysters, leaving the liquor in the shell with the meat. Arrange the open oysters, without their top shells, on your serving plate. Top each open oyster with *chicharrón* crumbs.

If desired, sprinkle the cilantro on top of the mignonette sauce. Put the mignonette bowl in the center of the serving plate. Serve immediately.

Chicharrones

½ onion, peeled

1 garlic bulb, top removed

1 jalapeño chile

1 pound fresh pork skin, fat removed, cut into pieces about as big as your hand

3 teaspoons salt

½ cup white vinegar

4 cups frying fat (lard is traditional), or as needed

Chicharrones are a delicious snack of fried and salted pork skins widely enjoyed throughout Mexico. In U.S. cities, you typically find them in the salty-snacks aisle of Mexican grocery stores or in convenience stores in Latino neighborhoods. The bags range from locally made products with a small ingredient bill (pork skins, lard, salt, spices) to mass-produced brands containing a lot of preservatives and other chemicals.

The best-tasting *chicharrones*, of course, are ones you've made yourself. For most people, the trickiest part of making them in the United States will be finding the raw pork skin to fry. Look for a meat counter that still has human butchers working at it— which, once again, may be easiest to find in your nearest Latino neighborhood.

When *chicharrones* get stale, you can crush them and use them in recipes as an umami-rich alternative to panko crumbs.

Note: The pork skins take several days to dry out after being initially cooked but before frying. You'll need to plan ahead for this one, but it's worth it!

Fill a stockpot over half full with water and add the onion, garlic, and jalapeño. Put the pot over high heat and bring the contents to a boil.

When the water starts to boil, add the pork skin. Put a heat-tolerant plate directly on top of the water to keep the pork skins fully submerged while cooking. Boil for 90 minutes. Check to see if the pork is fully cooked by cutting off a small piece; when it is ready, it will be soft and not sticky. You should probably taste it, too, both to double-check that it is done and to sample the delicious pork skin.

In a small bowl or measuring cup, whisk 2 teaspoons of the salt into the vinegar using a fork. Put the pork skin onto wire racks over sheet pans or plates and brush the skins on both sides with the vinegar-salt mixture. Put the racks in the fridge, uncovered, and let the skins sit for 3 to 4 days, until they are dry and crispy.

When the pork skins are dry, they are ready to fry. Put the frying fat in a wok or Dutch oven, and heat until it is stable at 350°F. (see page 128). If the fat isn't deep enough to submerge the skin, add more fat and bring it to temperature.

When the fat is ready, drop in the pork skin, one piece at a time. It should puff and curl. Move it around as needed for it to fully cook. Typically, each piece takes about 5 minutes. If the pork skin starts to turn dark brown, that's too long.

Remove each piece from the fat, place on a drying rack, and season with the remaining 1 teaspoon salt. Let the pieces cool. Stored at room temperature, the *chicharrones* will keep for a few days, but they will have the best texture the first day.

Shrimp, octopus, and chicharrón quesadillas

1 poblano chile, stemmed and seeded

1 small tomato, stemmed

1 onion, peeled

1 tablespoon neutral cooking oil, such as canola oil

1 garlic clove, peeled and minced

6 ounces Basic Octopus (page 119), chopped into ½-inch chunks

6 ounces peeled and deveined medium shrimp (sizes 36/40 or 41/50 are ideal)

1 teaspoon kosher salt

¼ cup butter

6 flour tortillas (see page 38)

2 cups grated mozzarella cheese (or other easily melted cheese)

1 cup chicharrones (see page 114), crumbled into pieces smaller than ½ inch

For serving

2 limes, cut into wedges

Tomatillo/Avocado Sauce (page 78; optional)

Tangy Red Salsa (page 136; optional)

One of my favorite stops for lunch near my home is the restaurant Muelle 3, a tiny dockside café at the Ensenada harbor. They offer traditional seafood dishes, such as oysters on the half shell and ceviche, and they also feature some more far-out creations. One of their signatures is "D'Harina," a quesadilla with a seafood mix including shrimp and octopus, topped with fried pork rinds. It's one of many Baja dishes that mix local shellfish with umami-forward flavors of meat. Here's a recipe for a similar quesadilla that's pretty easy to make at home. I promise it will be a big hit with guests.

Dice the poblano into ¼-inch pieces and set aside.

Chop the tomato as small as you comfortably can, discarding the juice and seeds, and set aside.

Dice the onion to about the same size as the chile and set aside.

Warm the oil in a frying pan over medium-low heat. Add the onion and cook for 5 minutes, stirring as needed to prevent it from burning, until it has softened and turned somewhat translucent. Add the garlic and continue to cook for 3 minutes.

Turn the heat to medium and add the chopped chile. Add a little water at any time if the mixture starts to dry out. At some point, the chile and onion pieces will release their moisture and that will provide additional cooking liquid.

Cook the chile for 5 minutes. Then turn the heat to medium-high and add the tomato and octopus. Wait 2 minutes for the pan to heat up, add the shrimp, and season everything with the salt. Cook for 2 to 3 minutes, stirring and flipping the shrimp as needed for them to cook evenly. When done, the shrimp should be bright pink and white and opaque, not at all translucent. As soon as all the shrimp reach that state, remove the pan from the heat so that the shrimp don't overcook and become tough.

continued

Shrimp, octopus, and chicharrón quesadillas, continued

———————————

Melt 1 tablespoon of the butter in a separate frying pan over medium heat, making sure the bottom of the pan is generously coated. Put a tortilla in the pan, letting it cook until it has very lightly started to turn golden, about 30 seconds. Flip it over with tongs and sprinkle it with ⅓ cup of the grated mozzarella. As the cheese starts to melt, fold the tortilla, and cook the half moon–shaped tortilla first on one side and then the other, until the outside is a rich golden color, another minute or two.

Remove the tortilla from the pan and, using your fingers carefully so as not to burn them, open the quesadilla. Spoon a large portion of the shrimp-octopus mixture onto the cheese side of the tortilla and then top it with a small handful of *chicharrones*. Fold the tortilla back into a quesadilla, with the top just resting on the filling—there should be enough filling in the tortilla that it won't fully close. Cover the quesadilla with a towel to keep it warm.

Repeat the process with each tortilla.

Cut the quesadillas in half so each piece is a gooey quarter circle. Serve with the lime wedges and tomatillo/avocado sauce or red salsa.

Basic octopus

¼ cup kosher salt

12 ounces octopus, cleaned

Octopus needs to boil for quite a while to make it tender inside, but for a lot of dishes you also want it to have a slightly crispy exterior. For that reason, we usually boil it first and then, when needed, crisp it in a pan or fryer immediately before serving. This recipe is for that first cooking. When done, the octopus will be soft enough to eat cold, while also suitable for searing.

Fill a large pot with water and add the salt. Bring to a rolling boil.

Add the octopus to the pot and cook for 1 hour. It should be as tender as the skin between your thumb and forefinger. If it's not at least that tender, keep cooking until it is.

Make an ice bath by putting ice and tap water in a bowl big enough to hold the octopus. Remove the octopus from the pot, put it in the ice bath, and let it sit for 10 minutes.

Once the octopus has cooled completely, remove it from the ice bath and strain off any excess water. Use in a recipe immediately or store it in the fridge for up to 5 days.

Crab machaca tacos
(machaca de jaiba)

5 serrano chiles

1 jalapeño chile

1 chile güero (aka yellow chile or Santa Fe Grande)

4 teaspoons butter

2 onions, peeled and diced small

2 tomatoes, stemmed and diced small

6 bay leaves

2 garlic cloves, peeled

1 pound cooked crabmeat

1 teaspoon kosher salt

4 teaspoons black pepper

½ bunch cilantro, stem bases removed, chopped

For serving

8 flour tortillas (see page 38)

1 lime, cut into wedges

Tomatillo/Avocado Sauce (page 78; optional)

Tangy Red Salsa (page 136; optional)

Machaca made from tender local crabmeat is something you'll see often in Baja, particularly in the southern half—the state of Baja California Sur. This so-called machaca is not actually dried and rehydrated the way beef machaca is; instead, the recipe gets its name from the mixing of chiles and onions with shredded crab, in the typical style of beef machaca. Nowadays, I sometimes see this dish accompanied by corn tortillas, but I find that the flavor of warm flour tortillas better complements the sweet, butter-cooked crab.

If you live somewhere in the United States or Canada with delicious local crab this is a great recipe you can work into your repertoire. It'll probably be a little different from what your neighbors make!

Remove and discard the stems, seeds, pith, and ribs from all the chiles. Dice the chiles small.

Melt 2 teaspoons of the butter in a large pan over medium heat. Add the onions and cook until they become partially translucent, about 5 minutes.

Add the serranos, jalapeño, and chile güero to the pan and let them cook for about 8 minutes, until all the chiles are soft. Then add the tomatoes and cook for 3 minutes, or until they are fully cooked through. Remove the pan from the heat and set aside.

In another pan, melt the remaining 2 teaspoons butter over medium heat. Add the bay leaves and garlic, followed by the crabmeat. Season the meat with the salt and pepper. Add a little bit of water to the pan to ensure the crab stays moist. Cook the crabmeat for 3 minutes, stirring as it heats, so it absorbs the aromatics of the garlic and bay leaves.

Add the chile-onion mixture from the first pan to the crabmeat. Cook, continuing to stir, for 3 minutes, ensuring all the ingredients are fully jumbled together. Continue to add water if needed at any point so that the ingredients don't burn. Add the cilantro and cook for 3 minutes more.

Remove the garlic cloves and bay leaves and put the crabmeat on a serving plate. Encourage your diners to assemble their own tacos with the flour tortillas and lime wedges, accompanied by tomatillo/avocado sauce and/or red salsa.

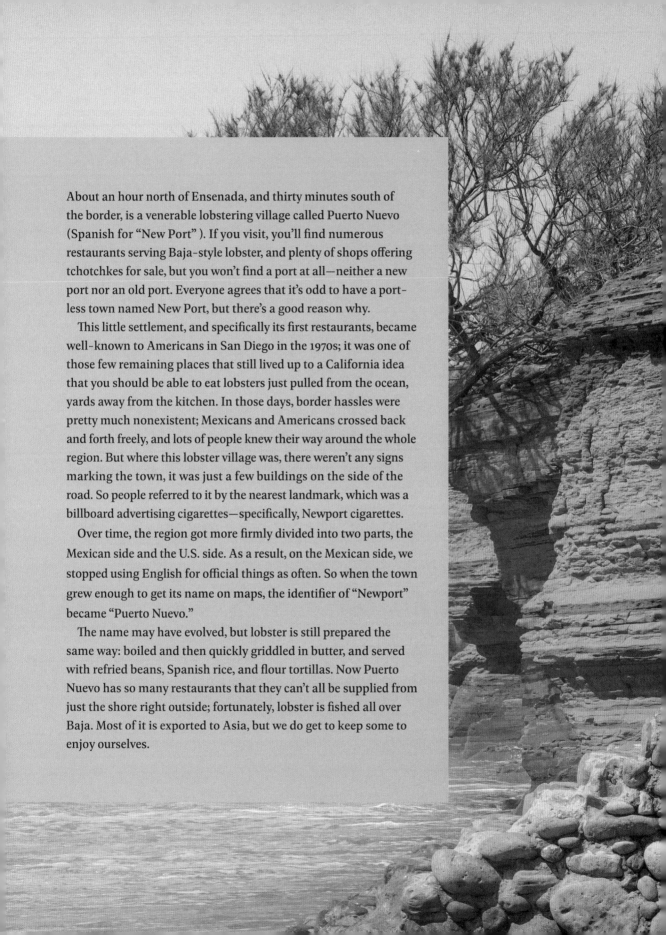

About an hour north of Ensenada, and thirty minutes south of the border, is a venerable lobstering village called Puerto Nuevo (Spanish for "New Port"). If you visit, you'll find numerous restaurants serving Baja-style lobster, and plenty of shops offering tchotchkes for sale, but you won't find a port at all—neither a new port nor an old port. Everyone agrees that it's odd to have a port-less town named New Port, but there's a good reason why.

This little settlement, and specifically its first restaurants, became well-known to Americans in San Diego in the 1970s; it was one of those few remaining places that still lived up to a California idea that you should be able to eat lobsters just pulled from the ocean, yards away from the kitchen. In those days, border hassles were pretty much nonexistent; Mexicans and Americans crossed back and forth freely, and lots of people knew their way around the whole region. But where this lobster village was, there weren't any signs marking the town, it was just a few buildings on the side of the road. So people referred to it by the nearest landmark, which was a billboard advertising cigarettes—specifically, Newport cigarettes.

Over time, the region got more firmly divided into two parts, the Mexican side and the U.S. side. As a result, on the Mexican side, we stopped using English for official things as often. So when the town grew enough to get its name on maps, the identifier of "Newport" became "Puerto Nuevo."

The name may have evolved, but lobster is still prepared the same way: boiled and then quickly griddled in butter, and served with refried beans, Spanish rice, and flour tortillas. Now Puerto Nuevo has so many restaurants that they can't all be supplied from just the shore right outside; fortunately, lobster is fished all over Baja. Most of it is exported to Asia, but we do get to keep some to enjoy ourselves.

Puerto nuevo–style lobster

2 Pacific spiny lobsters, live

1 cup butter

1 teaspoon kosher salt

For serving

Spanish Rice (page 127)

Refried beans (see page 32)

Flour tortillas (see page 38)

Charred Green Salsa (page 31)

Our local lobsters are called Pacific spinys, and they differ from the Maine lobsters found in U.S. restaurants in a very important way: ours don't have claws that you can crack and eat. Instead, they have an ample amount of meat in their bodies, along with the usual plump tail. The recipe here is based on the traditional way of cooking spinys in Baja; if you want to make it with an East Coast lobster, just stuff the claw meat into the body cavity after boiling (but before broiling). Probably no one will even be the wiser.

As with Maine lobsters, Pacific spinys are to be kept alive until the moment they are plunged into boiling water.

Bring a large stockpot of water to a rolling boil. While you are waiting for the water to boil, fill a large bowl with water and ice.

When the water in the pot is at a rolling boil, plunge each lobster into the pot headfirst. You don't need to cover the pot, as long as you keep it boiling. If the pot is big enough for multiple lobsters, it's fine to cook them in groups, but let the water recover to a full boil before putting the next lobster in. Cook each lobster for 8 minutes. When a lobster is cooked, its shell will be bright red. At that point, use tongs to move the lobster to the ice water bath in order to cool it.

Preheat the broiler to its maximum temperature.

Wait until the lobsters have cooled enough to comfortably handle them. Then, using a large serrated knife and/or shears, cut each lobster lengthwise into its right-side half and its left-side half.

Remove the lobsters' intestinal tract and lungs. Also take out the tomalley, which is the soft green substance inside the shell. This is edible, but because it serves as the animal's liver, it also stores some toxins. If you are using a lobster with claws, now is the time to crack the claws open and remove the meat. Place the claw meat somewhere convenient in the body cavity.

Gently melt the butter in a small saucepan over low heat, stirring in the salt with a fork or spoon.

Arrange the lobster halves onto sheet pans, meat-side up. Brush the lobsters' meat generously with about half of the melted butter.

Put the buttered lobster halves under the broiler and cook for 3 minutes, until the meat is just opaque. If you can't fit all four halves in the broiler at once, just do them in two sets. It's not essential that they all come out of the broiler at exactly the same time.

When you remove the lobsters from the broiler, drizzle the remaining butter over each piece. Serve them alongside Spanish rice, refried beans, flour tortillas, and salsa.

Spanish rice

---

2 tomatoes, stemmed

½ yellow onion, peeled

1 garlic clove, peeled

1 teaspoon kosher salt

1 tablespoon cooking oil, such as canola oil, or as needed

1 cup uncooked white rice

1½ cups chicken broth

Spanish rice is well-known as a component of combination platters in beloved Mexican restaurants throughout the States. In Mexico, it's just one type of rice that we eat, but it's still a favorite. The restaurants in Puerto Nuevo, which cater to both Mexicans and Americans, typically serve Spanish rice as part of their lobster feasts.

Cut the tomatoes in half, and cut the onion into two equal pieces. Put the tomatoes, onion, garlic, and salt in a blender or food processor and blend until smooth. Set this mixture aside.

Cover the bottom of a pot with the cooking oil and place over medium heat. Once the oil is hot, add the rice, stirring it slowly and constantly so it doesn't burn. Keep cooking until the rice is golden brown, about 5 minutes.

Add the tomato mixture to the rice and cook for 2 minutes, continuing to stir constantly.

Add the chicken broth to the pot and cover. Keeping the heat low enough to avoid burning the rice, cook at a simmer for 30 to 45 minutes, until the rice has absorbed all the liquid and has a light texture. Serve immediately.

ON DEEP-FRYING AT HOME

Deep frying—think of french fries and fish and chips—is something that is easiest to do in a commercial kitchen outfitted for that purpose. However, you can get good results deep-frying at home, even without dedicated frying equipment.

The first thing you'll require is a well-suited vessel. It needs to be deep enough to easily submerge your items to fry with room to spare, and narrow enough that you don't have to use an excessive amount of frying fat. Many home cooks use a wok or a wok-shaped pot for deep-frying: the narrow bottom of the wok allows you to use the minimum necessary amount of frying fat, and the wide skirt offers some protection from splatter. Other options include using a Dutch oven or a cast-iron kettle.

An important consideration is that the vessel be of heavy construction. This is not just so that it doesn't suddenly get too hot to handle (although that is helpful); it is also so that the pot maintains a very stable temperature even as the state of its contents fluctuate. For instance, you don't want the pot to immediately go cold as soon as you dunk a piece of fish in it. Maintaining a very consistent oil temperature is essential to good frying, and a heavy pot will help you do that.

Once you have your pot, you need to fill it with frying fat. In Baja, probably the most characteristic frying fat is lard. We use it for frying the fish in fish tacos and also for making *chicharrones*, among other things. Lard has a reputation in the United States for being unhealthful, but if you have clean lard from a great farmer, it's probably a better choice than any industrial oil. With lard, the trick is to be careful with its temperature, as it has a slightly lower smoke point (370°F) than some other frying fats. Smoke point is an indication of the temperature at which the oil will begin to burn off, and burned oil will make your food taste bad.

Many restaurants in the United States use canola oil or soybean oil as their frying fats. Both have a fairly high smoke point (400°F and 450°F, respectively) and, as key outputs of the industrial food system, are quite cheap to the consumer, particularly when bought in large quantities. Other great options include peanut oil (with a smoke point of 450°F), which in deep-frying doesn't make the food taste particularly peanut-y; rice bran oil (490°F), which tends to impart an enjoyably unctuous texture; and safflower oil (510°F).

Two final pieces of equipment are a deep-frying thermometer (also known as a candy thermometer), and, optionally, a mesh splatter screen you can lay over the top of the pan to keep from getting hot oil on yourself or your things. The frying thermometer affixes to the side of the pot by means of a clip, and you'll keep an eye on it constantly to ensure that you are frying at the desired temperature.

An important technique to know is the "double fry." To use this method, you cook your item all the way through and then remove it from the oil. At least a few minutes later, once the item has fully drained, you fry it again, just long enough to crisp the outside and make the center warm. This process tends to extract excess moisture from the inside of the food, helping it crisp in a delightful way. On the streets of Ensenada, you'll see the cooks at the fish-taco stands using this same process. It also works very well for french fries and crispy fried chicken; cooks making those items often like to raise the temperature of the oil for the second fry and make it shorter, to add even more crispiness.

Beer-battered fish tacos
with cabbage and white sauce

For the beer batter

2½ cups all-purpose flour, plus more for drying the fish

⅔ cup cornstarch

1 teaspoon baking powder

1 tablespoon yellow mustard

¼ cup chopped fresh Mexican oregano

One 12-ounce bottle beer (preferably a Mexican pilsner such as Pacifico or Bohemia Clara)

2 to 4 cups frying oil (lard is traditional, but any frying oil will do)

1 pound shark or meaty white fish such as cod or halibut, cut into 10 pieces, each between 1 and 2 ounces and about the size of a lumberjack's finger, or 1 pound large shrimp (no smaller than 26/30 size)

For serving

10 corn tortillas (see page 142)

½ head green cabbage, shredded

Baja White Sauce (page 137)

Tangy Red Salsa (page 136)

Pico de Gallo (page 133)

4 limes, cut into wedges

Fish tacos—batter-fried fillets, topped with cabbage, white sauce, pico de gallo, and red salsa—are possibly the most well-known street food of northern Baja. In Ensenada, fishermen unload from their *panga* boats hauls of premium fish such as yellowtail and grouper, plus bycatch including small sharks such as *angelito* (angel shark) and *cazón* (dogfish). The shark fillets sell very cheaply on the local market, and as a result, fish tacos—made from this exquisitely fresh fish—sell for around a dollar on the streets in town.

In the United States, unless you live near a commercial fishing operation, you probably won't have a local surplus of small sharks. But you can make a comparably delicious—albeit much more expensive—version using a meaty white fish such as halibut. Or, if you have a good source of shrimp, you can authentically use that; most fish-taco stands in Ensenada also offer the same taco with fried shrimp.

When you make these at home, here's one little trick to replicate authentic Ensenada street-food style—first, fry all of your fish strips and then, right before you put each piece of fish in a tortilla to serve, dunk that piece back in the hot oil for thirty seconds or so. That second time in the frying pot will crisp its outside and give it the "fresh from the fryer" sensation that really pops!

To make the beer batter: Combine the flour, cornstarch, baking powder, mustard, and oregano in a large bowl. Mix well.

Add the beer to the bowl and stir to combine. (Depending on the flour and other circumstances, you may need to adjust the amount a little from what's stated in the ingredient list. You know you have the right amount of beer mixed in when you start to see small reflective ribbons in the batter. The best situation is if you need just a tiny bit more than one bottle of beer, so you have almost a full bottle remaining that you then must drink while cooking.)

continued

Push the batter through a fine-mesh strainer into a small casserole dish or serving-size bowl. Discard the solids.

Put the frying oil in a wok or Dutch oven. You will need enough oil to fully cover the battered fish pieces. Heat the oil to 365°F (see page 128). Line a plate with paper towels.

Dry the raw fish pieces with paper towels, then lightly flour them, just enough to wick away any remaining moisture.

One by one, dredge each piece of fish in the batter. The batter should fully coat the fish and hang off it a little. Working in batches as needed so as not to crowd the pan, submerge the fish in the oil and fry the pieces until golden brown, 4 to 8 minutes. Remove each piece of fish from the oil and set it on the paper towel–lined plate.

Heat the tortillas on your grill or in a pan. (You can use a *comal* or *plancha* if you have one.) Don't use any oil on the tortillas.

Place one piece of fish in each tortilla. If using shrimp, use two to three per tortilla, making sure to distribute them more or less equally across each taco. For maximum authenticity, let each diner apply the cabbage, white sauce, red salsa, and pico de gallo to their own tacos according to their taste. Put a lime wedge on the side of each plate when serving.

Pico de gallo

Juice of 2 limes

3 tablespoons extra-virgin olive oil

½ bunch cilantro

1 serrano chile

1 onion, peeled

2 tomatoes, stemmed

Kosher salt

Black pepper

Pico de gallo is a fresh-made salsa that doesn't have a lot of liquid, so it's particularly good for topping tacos without making them soggy. Sometimes you also see it called *salsa fresca*, which means "fresh sauce."

With a fork, mix the lime juice and olive oil in a small bowl or glass and then set aside.

Remove the heavy stem bases of the cilantro. Chop the remaining leaves and thin stems as fine as you can without trying particularly hard. (You wouldn't want any stress to make its way into the dish.)

Remove the stem of the chile. If you'd like to make sure the pico de gallo isn't very spicy, also slice the chile lengthwise and remove the seeds, ribs, and pith. (Be sure not to touch your eyes afterward or it will burn!) After the chile is stemmed and optionally de-ribbed and seeded, cut it into a very fine dice.

Cut the onion and tomatoes into pieces ⅓ inch per side or less; I think ¼ inch per side is ideal.

Put the tomatoes, onion, and chile in a large bowl and toss them together, seasoning with salt and pepper. Add the lime juice mixture and toss a little more. Use immediately or keep in the fridge for up to 1 week.

Tangy red salsa

2 dried arbol chiles

4 dried guajillo chiles

¼ cup neutral cooking oil, such as canola oil or grapeseed oil, or as needed

½ red onion, peeled and quartered

8 garlic cloves, peeled

1 large tomato (or 2 small tomatoes), stemmed and quartered

Juice of 3 limes

¼ bunch cilantro

1 teaspoon kosher salt

1 teaspoon black pepper

In the carts, stands, and restaurants throughout Baja, you'll almost always find a fresh-made spicy red sauce ready for you to spoon on any item you like. This sauce goes alongside pretty much anything and everything. You'll also find countless delicious ways to make a salsa like this; here's one good recipe.

Stem all the chiles and then pour out and discard the seeds. You don't have to worry about getting every last seed removed; it's fine if some end up in the salsa.

Warm the cooking oil in a frying pan over medium-low heat. Make sure the oil is at least ¹⁄₁₆ inch deep—a little more than just a coating.

Once the oil is hot, add the chiles. Stir them continually so they cook evenly until they are soft, 5 to 10 minutes. Add the onion and garlic and continue to stir lightly about 5 minutes more, enough to soften them and infuse the oil with their flavor. Add the tomato and cook just until warm, about 3 minutes more.

Remove the pan from the heat and put its contents in a blender or food processor. Add the lime juice and cilantro and blend until smooth. If the consistency stays lumpier than you would like, add water as needed. Season with salt and pepper and blend a little longer.

If you like a very smooth salsa, you can strain the mixture through a fine-mesh sieve at this point.

Let the salsa cool to room temperature. Serve immediately or store in the fridge for up to 1 week.

Baja white sauce

½ cup mayonnaise

½ cup Mexican crema
(or ¼ cup cultured buttermilk
and ¼ cup heavy cream)

Juice of 1 lime

½ teaspoon black pepper

½ teaspoon kosher salt

In my opinion, white sauce is the distinctive flavor that makes a fish taco *a fish taco*. A lot of chefs, particularly those outside of Baja, like to showcase their skills by putting a fancier sauce over the battered fish in the tacos they serve. That's all good, but it doesn't taste like home. I like this simple mix of mayonnaise and crema.

This recipe calls for a whisk, but it's fine to use a blender or food processor instead, if you don't mind the extra cleaning.

Put the mayonnaise, crema, lime juice, and pepper in a bowl and whisk. Add the salt, adjusting to taste, while whisking as needed.

The final sauce should be thin enough to easily spoon (or to dispense from a squeeze bottle as they do at the taco stands) but thick enough that, once dispensed, it sits firmly in place and doesn't run off the fish. (If you need to make it thinner, add lime juice, or crema. Alternatively, to make it firmer, add mayonnaise or heavy cream.)

Serve in a squeeze bottle or in a bowl with spoon. White sauce will keep in the fridge for up to 1 week.

ON MASA

If you've ever eaten even one dish of Mexican food, there's a good chance you've eaten a corn tortilla. Or a tostada. Or a tamal, or sopes, or gorditas, or maybe even something more exotic such as a *huarache* or a *tlacayo* or *pozole* or a sweet glass of *atole*.

What all these foods have in common is that they are made from corn. Specifically, they are made from masa, which is corn that has undergone a certain alkalization process. The word we use to describe corn that has undergone this process is *nixtamal*—a word given to us by the Aztecs. The process itself is usually called nixtamalization.

Nixtamalization has multiple benefits. It frees up some key nutrients in the corn that otherwise would not be bio-available. It also makes the corn kernels puffy and soft, and easier to then grind into various cakes and sheets, or to mix with fats or liquids. Most notably, it makes maize—not the sweet corn that Americans eat in the summer, but the dry kind of corn that gets otherwise fed to livestock or processed into ethanol—taste great.

In U.S. English, nixtamalized corn kernels are called "hominy." Since we are describing corn in the context of Mexican food, in this book we use *nixtamal* to describe the alkalinized corn kernels, and *masa* to describe the dough made from ground nixtamal.

Traditionally, nixtamal was made in individual Mexican households, where the kernels were then hand ground into masa against a stone plate called a *metate*. With this process, to make a day's worth of tortillas for just one family could take hours and hours. Now, almost everyone in Mexico buys their corn tortillas pre-made.

While some people in both the United States and Mexico are lucky enough to live near a tortilleria that makes great tortillas, their scarcity has ignited a movement of reviving small-scale tortilla production, sometimes also from preindustrial corn. It's becoming increasingly more common in the United States to find small tortillerias, Mexican grocery stores, neighborhood restaurants, and home cooks who know how to source good maize, nixtamalize it, and grind it into masa for tortillas, tamales, and more.

If you have access to these kinds of tortillas, most of the time it makes more sense to buy them rather than make them. Additionally, tortillerias like these often sell fresh-made masa dough (usually called *masa para tortillas* to distinguish it from a masa with fat and spices added, which is used to make tamales). You can buy *masa para tortillas* and use it to make fresh-pressed tortillas, sopes, tostadas, or even prepare it for use in tamales. (We've included some information in the Purchasing Notes, page 251, that might help you with sourcing.)

Working a *metate* for hours is not a practical option for many people, and mechanically grinding masa is most easily done with large-scale equipment. Grinding nixtamal at home can be done but it poses some challenges. You will need one of three tools.

A mill (*molino* in Spanish): This tool is usually hand-operated and designed for wet grinding. You may be able to find it at a Mexican market or another specialty store. Ask for a *molino para nixtamal.*

An electric nixtamal grinder (such as the Nixtamatic) or electric mixer attachment with plates: This tool is specifically made for grinding masa and is typically purchased online.

A food processor: If you grind with a food processor, you have to grind the masa while it is still very wet—too wet to form into tortillas. So, after grinding the masa, you will need to thicken it, and for that, it is easiest to use a small bag of *masa harina* purchased from the store.

As for the ingredients in masa, there are only two, but both are unfamiliar to many American home cooks.

The first ingredient is called "cal." Sometimes it's called "culinary lime," "pickling lime," or "slaked lime." Its chemical name is calcium hydroxide. In the kitchen, cal is like a very alkaline salt. Note that, while food-grade cal is considered safe and many cooks handle cal without gloves, we recommend that you avoid getting it on your skin or eyes or ingesting it. For tips on finding cal, see page 253.

The other ingredient is corn—specifically "field corn," which is different from the corn you buy in the grocery store. (That grocery-store corn is called "sweet corn.") Field corn, which is sold as dried kernels, is typically a commodity bought in very large quantities by industrial-scale businesses. However, recently, it's become possible to buy small amounts of high-quality field corn, often of heirloom varieties, specifically marketed to home cooks making nixtamal. We've listed some purveyors of these products on page 252.

One important consideration to keep in mind is that cooking and soaking time vary dramatically with the type of corn you use. And, there are many, many varieties of corn you can use for this, so there are many possible "right answers" for cooking and soaking time. I've made nixtamal with corn that required as much as twelve hours of boiling and two days of soaking! However, more typical is an hour of boiling followed by an overnight soaking. That is a good place to start if your corn didn't come with instructions.

Last, while we really want you to eat the highest-quality corn tortillas you can, here's a dirty secret: Many people prefer their fish tacos made with bland factory-made corn tortillas, because they don't overpower the mild flavor of the fish. So, don't sweat it if that's what you end up using.

Masa
for corn tortillas, tostaditas, sopes, and more

7 grams cal, aka "culinary lime" or calcium hydroxide (see page 253)

1 pound dried heirloom corn (see page 252)

Small bag of masa harina (optional; only necessary if you are using a food processor to grind the masa)

Due to the forces of industrialization and for other reasons, even in Mexico, many times the local corn tortillas are not very good. The same is true in American supermarkets. In both countries, you can alternatively buy a just-add-water tortilla dough called *masa harina* and make tortillas at home with it. It's probably unsurprising that those tortillas are not very delicious either.

However, if your only good masa option is to make it yourself, don't despair! It is possible to do everything you need in your own kitchen. (Feel free to refer back to "On Masa" on page 138.)

Once you've made the nixtamal and ground it into masa, you still have many options of what to do with it. In this recipe, we give instructions for pressing masa into tortillas, and, optionally, cooking those tortillas into tostadas to serve alongside some of the dishes in this book. Note that, for this recipe, amounts are given in weight instead of volume. Use a digital kitchen scale on its "grams" setting to measure the correct amount of cal.

Note: If you scale this recipe, keep the weights of the cal and corn at the same ratio. The amount of water used is not particularly important as long as it sufficient to hold all the other ingredients, with plenty of room left over.

Fill a large stockpot with water. (Aim for about twice the volume of the corn you have, so that, later, when you put the corn in the pot, the kernels will be covered with twice their height in water.) Add the cal to the water and bring it to a rolling boil.

Add the corn to the pot and let it cook for 1 hour. You may need to adjust this time significantly depending on the corn, so don't worry if it turns out that you really need to cook it for several hours. Test to see if the corn is done by rubbing a kernel between your thumb and forefinger; if the skin detaches easily, it's done cooking.

continued

Masa, continued

Once the corn is done cooking, remove the pot from the heat and cover loosely with plastic wrap. Let soak overnight at room temperature. Again, it's possible that the required soaking time may be quite a bit longer than this, depending on your type of corn, but overnight is a good starting point.

The next day, wash the corn thoroughly with running water, using a colander. When you are washing the corn, the kernel skins will easily come off. That is what you want; just discard the skins. Your masa will be smoother with the skins gone. However, if some of the skins stay in the mix, that will give the masa a more rustic quality. Either way is awesome. Once the corn is fully washed, you are ready to grind the nixtamal into masa.

If you have a dedicated masa grinder, follow the instructions provided with the grinder. Remember to add water as needed to keep the masa loose and soft enough to work with, but not so wet that it becomes runny. The consistency you want is like potting clay—a little bit denser than bread dough or pasta dough. It should be soft enough to mold without working hard, while still holding its shape once molded. It should not stick to your hands.

If you are using a food processor, you will be grinding it in batches in the bowl, using the basic blade. Fill the bowl about one-fourth full of corn, add a little water, and start the motor while continuing to pour water in as need to facilitate the grinding. By the time you grind the masa to a smooth consistency, it will almost certainly be so wet as to be runny. There are some time-intensive ways to dry it out, but the easiest thing to do is to mix it in a bowl with some masa harina from the store, which will soak up the excess water.

Once you have ground all your masa, you can put it in a bag and store it in the fridge for a couple weeks, continuing to make tortillas and more with it as needed.

To make tortillas, first preheat your cooking surface. Cast iron works great for this, but you can use any nonstick surface that gets very hot. Aim for 450°F. (You can oil the surface a little if needed to keep it nonstick, but use only the minimum needed amount; we are not sautéing the tortilla, we are dry-cooking.)

Weigh out 1 ounce of masa and shape it into a ball. Using a tortilla press (or your hands if you are patient and talented), shape the masa into a flat disc, about as thick as a poker chip and 4 to 6 inches across.

Using your fingers, deposit the disc on the cooking surface. Let it sit for 45 seconds, flip it, cook it another 45 seconds, flip it again, and then cook it 10 to 15 seconds or more if needed. If everything happens perfectly, the tortilla will puff up like a blowfish toward the end of its cooking, but plenty of tortillas don't puff and are still great. So don't get hung up on that.

When the tortilla is done, keep it warm between two towels or in a tortilla basket. (Or just sprinkle some salt on it and eat it while standing over the stove. That is also a traditional move.) Repeat with more masa to make the number of tortillas you require.

Once you have tortillas, if you want to make tostadas, you have two options. First, you can deep-fry them, using the frying method given on page 128, and let them cool on paper towels to wick away any excess oil. Or, you can bake the cooked tortillas in a 350°F oven, flat on a sheet pan with no oil, for about 20 minutes.

Gobernador tacos
(shrimp, poblano, and cheese tacos)

4 teaspoons neutral cooking oil, such as canola oil

1 onion, peeled and diced

1 garlic clove, peeled and minced

2 poblano chiles, stems removed, cut into ¼-inch-wide strips

8 corn tortillas (see page 142)

Juice of 3 limes

1 slice bacon, diced small

8 ounces peeled and deveined medium shrimp (preferably sizes 36/40 or 41/50; if you have bigger shrimp, slice them in half lengthwise)

1 teaspoon kosher salt

1 cup Queso Asadero cheese (see "Purchasing Notes," page 251; if not available, substitute Teleme or Monterey Jack)

For serving

2 limes, cut into wedges

Tangy Red Salsa (page 136; optional)

Tacos de Gobernador are a cultural import that crossed the Sea of Cortez. They come from Sinaloa, where they are supposedly named in honor of a local mayor who liked his shrimp tacos topped with cheese and chiles. The name of the politician is lost to time, but the name of the taco has become very popular in northern Baja California and also across the border in San Diego and Los Angeles.

As a fairly new folk food, *gobernadores* tend to be different any place you have them. In fact, I think there are as many versions as there are mayors! The one constant is that they include shrimp. Sometimes they also incorporate smoked marlin. They usually include some kind of mild chiles. More often than not, cheese, which is included here, is melted on them. This recipe also integrates a little bacon, giving it a surf-and-turf feel that is a signature of contemporary Baja food.

Warm 3 teaspoons of the oil in a frying pan over medium-low heat. Add the onion and cook for 5 minutes, stirring gently. Add the garlic and continue to cook for 3 minutes. (If, at any time during the cooking process, the items in the pan dry out at all, deglaze the pan with some lime juice, scraping up the browned bits with a wooden spoon, and continue.) Turn the heat to medium and add the chiles. Cook for 10 minutes, or until the chiles are thoroughly cooked.

At this point, warm a separate frying pan over medium heat and add the remaining 1 teaspoon oil. Interleaved with finishing the rest of the recipe, heat each tortilla in the oil-coated pan for about 20 seconds per side, just long enough to make them the slightest bit golden but still pliable, and put between two towels to stay warm and wick away any excess oil.

continued

Gobernador tacos, continued

Once the chiles have cooked for 10 minutes, pour the lime juice on the ingredients in the pan. Add the diced bacon to the pan and turn the heat to medium-high. When the pan has heated up and the bacon has started to turn color, add the shrimp and use the salt to season everything in the pan. Cook for 2 to 3 minutes, stirring and flipping the shrimp as necessary to cook them evenly. The shrimp should be bright pink and white and opaque. If they are still translucent, cook them a little longer.

Sprinkle the cheese over everything in the pan and turn the heat to low. Continue stirring until the cheese is melted. Remove the pan from the heat. Distribute the cheesy shrimp mixture equally among the tortillas, making a plate full of tacos. Serve along with the lime wedges and red salsa, if desired.

Mixed seafood stew
(estofado de mariscos)

---

1 to 2 pounds yellowtail
or tuna fillet

6 clams (see Note)

½ stalk celery

1 carrot, peeled

1 onion, peeled

1 tablespoon neutral cooking
oil, such as canola oil

3 garlic cloves, peeled

2 cups white wine

1 cup white vinegar

6 mussels

2 spiny lobsters, live

For the sauce

2 onions, peeled

2 tomatoes, stemmed

3 garlic cloves, peeled

2 teaspoons neutral cooking
oil, such as canola oil

10 dried pasilla chiles,
stemmed

¼ cup butter

4 cups Seafood Broth
(page 152), warmed

I think every area in the world with a seafood tradition has its own type of mixed seafood stew. Mexico has *siete mares*; San Francisco famously invented cioppino, inspired by the Italian *ciuppin*. Commercial fishing villages in the remote beaches of Baja Sur even have their own take on *ciuppin* called, in Spanish, *chopín*. With *chopín* in mind, here's a delicious Baja-style mixed seafood stew that you can make from lobster, clams, mussels, and yellowtail or tuna, all of which are fairly widely available to American cooks. You can garnish with any herbs you have on hand—a little bit of color adds a nice touch.

Note: Clean the clams using the method on page 94. Rinse the shells and set them aside; you will use them when serving the dish.

Dice the fish fillet into pieces a little bigger than 1 inch per side. Fine chop the clam meat and set it aside. Chop the celery, carrot, and onion into 1-inch dice.

Fill a large bowl with ice and water to make an ice bath.

Warm the oil in a medium pot over medium-high heat. Add the celery, carrot, onion, and garlic and cook for 4 minutes. Then add 6 cups water, the white wine, and vinegar. Turn the heat to high and bring the water to a boil. Drop the mussels into the pot and let them boil until they pop open, about 5 minutes. As each mussel pops open, fetch it from the pot using a basket spoon, and put in the ice bath. If any mussels stubbornly refuse to open, that means they have gone bad. Discard them. Once all the mussels are removed, discard the contents of the pot.

Fill a different large pot with water and bring it to a boil. Put the lobsters in the pot for 8 minutes, then remove the lobsters and put them in the ice bath with the mussels.

When the lobsters have cooled, split the lobster shells and remove the meat, discarding the goopy liquid inside. Set the meat aside, rinse the shells, and set the shells aside.

continued

To make the sauce: Preheat the broiler. Halve the onions and tomatoes and put them on a sheet pan along with the garlic. Put the sheet pan under the broiler until all the ingredients are heavily charred, about 5 minutes. Put the charred ingredients in a blender or food processor.

Warm the oil in a small sauté pan over medium-high heat. Add the dried chiles and cook until they inflate, stirring and adjusting the heat as necessary so they don't burn. It should take about 5 minutes. Add the chiles to the blender and puree into a liquid sauce, adding water as needed to thin it out. You want something that you can easily spoon onto the top of a bowl of soup.

Melt the butter in a small pan over medium-low heat. Add the lobster meat and stir, cooking for about 5 minutes, until the lobster is hot. Remove the lobster meat and set it aside. Turn the heat to medium-high. Add the clam meat and then the fish pieces and sear them so that the outside ¼ inch is fully cooked but the inside is totally rare.

Arrange the empty shells in a wide, shallow bowl. Put the lobster meat in the lobster shells. Put the clam meat and fish pieces inside the clamshells. Add the mussels in their shells. Pour the broth over the whole dish so that the tops of the shells rise above the top of the broth. Top the broth with the sauce. Give every diner an empty bowl for them to fill with their portion. Serve immediately.

Seafood broth

½ stalk celery

1 carrot, peeled

½ onion, peeled

1 tablespoon neutral cooking oil, such as canola oil

1 fish skeleton including head (or substitute shell of a large crab or lobster)

8 cups water

There's a culinary tradition in Mexico (among other places) in which you make a broth from the meat that will be featured in your main dish and serve that broth before the meal. So when you sit down to a feast of lamb *barbacoa*, you might first get a bowl of lamb consommé; while the *mariscos* stand is assembling your order, they might offer you a cup of seafood *caldo*.

In that spirit, here's a recipe for a quick stock you can make with the bones of any fish you've cooked, or from the shells of lobster or crab. You can serve it on its own before a meal, or use it instead of water in dishes such as Shrimp Meatballs in Tomato Sauce (page 155). It also serves as the base for the classic-style *mariscos* dish, Mixed Seafood Stew (page 149).

Chop the celery, carrot, and onion into 1-inch dice.

Warm the oil in a large pot over medium-high heat. Add the celery, carrot, and onion, and cook for 5 minutes, until they all soften. If they start to stick to the pot or burn, just deglaze the pot with a little water, scraping up the browned bits with a wooden spoon.

After 5 minutes, add the fish bones. Cook them for 3 minutes, again adding a little water as needed to keep the pot from drying out all the way. Then add the 8 cups water. Bring to a boil and then lower the heat and cook at a low simmer for 8 minutes.

When the mixture is done cooking, strain the liquid into a pitcher or serving bowl using a fine-mesh strainer. Discard the remaining (solid) ingredients. Use the broth immediately, refrigerate it for a day or two, or freeze it for use within a few months.

Shrimp meatballs
in tomato sauce

½ onion, peeled and halved

1 chipotle, from a can,
in marinade

1 pound shrimp, shelled and
deveined, heads removed

1 tablespoon panko crumbs

1 teaspoon black pepper

2 teaspoons kosher salt

1 tablespoon fresh curly
parsley, minced

1 egg white

2 tomatoes, stemmed

2 garlic cloves, peeled

1 tablespoon extra-virgin
olive oil

1 tablespoon tomato paste

2 bay leaves

4 cups water

2 tablespoons neutral cooking
oil, such as canola oil

In Mexico, we grow up eating meatballs—which we call
albondigas—as comfort food, just as people in the States do.
A variation of the dish that is associated with Baja is when the
meatballs are made from seafood, typically shrimp (any size
is fine). Whether they're made of seafood or meat, however,
we often eat *albondigas* in a light, tomato-y broth. I think the
combination of meatballs and tomato sauce is familiar enough
to Americans that even our Baja version will bring a warm glow.

Chop an onion quarter and the chipotle as fine as you can. Chop
the shrimp as fine as you can.

Put the shrimp in a bowl with the panko, black pepper, and
1 teaspoon of the salt. Add the fine-chopped onion and chipotle
and ½ tablespoon of the parsley. Use your hands to quickly mix
it together. Add the egg white and mix it again, this time until
you have a somewhat pasty, homogeneous mass.

Form the mixture into six meatballs of equal size. Place them
on a plate in the fridge. You'll get back to them in a few minutes.

Put the tomatoes, garlic, and remaining onion quarter in a blender
and liquefy the mixture.

Warm the olive oil in a large saucepan over medium heat, taking
care not to get it so hot that it smokes. When the olive oil is hot, add
the tomato paste to the pan. The paste should fry a little and, after
about 5 minutes, start to bubble. If it starts to blacken or burn at
any point, lower the heat.

Once the tomato paste has started to bubble, add the tomato
mixture from the blender, the bay leaves, and the remaining
1 teaspoon salt. Stir lightly and then add the water. Bring the
mixture to a boil and then turn the heat to a low simmer, stirring
occasionally.

continued

Shrimp meatballs, continued

After the sauce has simmered for 5 minutes, get out a new frying pan and pour the cooking oil into it. Place over very high heat. When the oil is hot, add the meatballs. You may have to cook them only one or two at a time so the pan and the oil maintain their heat.

Sear each meatball for about 1 minute, rotating them in the pan so that all sides of each meatball get browned. Once all the meatballs are seared, take them from the frying pan and put them in the saucepan with the tomato sauce. Cook for about 5 minutes more, until they are firm and the internal temperature of the meatballs reads 125°F as measured with an instant-read thermometer.

Place two or three meatballs in the center of each bowl. Pour the sauce over the meatballs, covering the bottom of the bowl but stopping before the meatballs are fully submerged. Sprinkle the reserved parsley over the filled bowls. Serve immediately.

When you talk to people in the Baja seafood industry, a couple of themes continually arise. The first is that this peninsula and its waters are special, with resources like few other places in the world. Just on the Sea of Cortez side, off of Loreto, there are more than nine hundred species of fish and one-third of the world's marine mammal species. That's why Jacques Cousteau called that area "the world's aquarium." It's amazing to visit and part of what makes the food here so special, too.

The other thing that everyone talks about, sometimes subtly, is that it's all changing, more rapidly than is widely known. The fish are disappearing. Harvests and catches are way down and falling more every year. Certain species of fish are being found where they've never been seen before. There's a sense that the oceans are in major disarray, and nothing the fishermen do can rehabilitate them. This isn't just a simply remedied problem of overfishing—although fishery management is a continually evolving challenge. A bigger problem comes from large-scale changes to the oceans themselves, as a result of the changing climate.

It's hard to know how long all the fish and shellfish we talk about here will be available to us—or to anybody. Baja has a lot of skilled and well-educated marine scientists and fishery managers who are doing their best to find ways for us to adapt to the circumstances. And there are aquatic farmers who are working to cultivate sustainable supplies of fish and shellfish. But it wasn't too long ago that the most prevalent food in Baja was *caguama*, or sea turtle, and that animal is now endangered. I hope that we don't look back in just a few decades and say the same thing about the rest of the seafood we eat.

Caguamanta
(old baja turtle stew, made with skate wing)

2 tablespoons dried
pasilla chiles

2 pounds fresh skate
wing fillets

1 tomato, stemmed

2 tablespoons tomato paste

1 teaspoon dried oregano

1 pinch ground cumin

1 teaspoon lard or other
cooking fat

2 garlic cloves, peeled

4 to 6 jalapeño chiles

½ stalk celery, diced

1 carrot, peeled and diced

⅓ pound medium shrimp,
peeled, with heads and
digestive tract removed

1 tablespoon kosher salt

½ cup red cabbage, shredded

Caguamanta is a variation of what may be the oldest Baja recipe, sea turtle stew. Turtle, called *caguama*, was plentiful and important sustenance for the indigenous people of Baja, and later for the European buccaneers who raided the sea lanes surrounding the peninsula.

As indigenous and Spanish culture meshed over the centuries, *caguama* became a signature of Baja. Street vendors and market stalls in the cities served turtle soup, while remote villages made flour tortillas from rendered turtle fat. Dozens, perhaps even hundreds, of other uses for different parts of the turtle were known across the region.

Through overfishing and poaching, sea turtles became gravely endangered, and it's been illegal to harvest them in Baja since 1990. As their population declined, alternatives arose, and now this dish is typically made with skate wing, *mantarraya* in Spanish. (This is a different fish from the giant fish known as manta ray in English.) Thus this particular mock turtle soup is called by the portmanteau *caguamanta*.

Caguamanta scales up well to feed large groups; it's often cooked in huge paella pans at festivals and parties. For more modest amounts, a rondeau pan (also known as a brazier) is perfect. A deep sauté pan or large saucepan also work fine.

Hydrate the pasilla chiles in a medium pot of boiling water for 10 minutes. Retrieve them with a slotted spoon or strainer, stem them, and set them aside. Cut the skate wing fillets into cubes about ½ inch thick. Bring a large pot of water to a boil. While the water is coming to a boil, fill a large bowl with water and ice cubes to make an ice bath. Once the water is boiling, put the skate wing cubes into the pot and immediately turn off the heat. Leave the skate wing in the water for 2 minutes. Then, using a slotted spoon or wire mesh, pull the pieces from the pot and immediately put them in the ice bath.

In the bowl of your blender, combine the tomato, tomato paste, oregano, cumin, and rehydrated chiles. Add just enough water to help the blender do its job. Blend until evenly mixed. Put the lard in a rondeau pan (or a deep sauté pan) and place over medium-low heat. As soon as the lard melts, add the garlic. Cook until the garlic begins to brown and then remove the cloves from the pan. Pour the contents of the blender into the saucepan and bring the mixture to a simmer, adjusting the heat as needed.

While the mixture is simmering, seed the jalapeños. Traditionally this dish is presented with whole chiles, but it is also not meant to be very spicy. For this reason, it is best to try to remove the pith, ribs, and seeds; the pith and ribs particularly contain a lot of the chile's heat. Make a T-shaped incision in the side of each chile, reach in with your knife, and remove as much of the pith, ribs, and seeds as you can.

After 5 minutes of simmering the tomato mixture, add the celery and carrot to the pan. Bring to a boil and then return it to a simmer.

Add the jalapeños and skate wing cubes. Simmer for 6 minutes, stirring as needed to keep everything cooking evenly. The skate wing cubes should be breaking down at this point.

Add the shrimp to the pan and then the salt, while stirring. Cook for about 4 minutes, until the shrimp is fully pink and no longer translucent. The final consistency of the dish as a whole should be thicker than porridge. This is a stew, but it lives more in the neighborhood of "casserole" and less in the vicinity of "soup." By the time the dish is served, the skate wing should have broken down into shreds.

Ladle the stew into bowls, making sure each gets a whole jalapeño. Garnish with the red cabbage and serve.

3

WINE COUNTRY

California winemaking, now famous for its products from Napa Valley, Sonoma County, and the Central Coast, began in Loreto in 1701. It moved north over the following decades in tandem with the Spanish missionaries who fostered it.

Nowadays, winemaking in Baja is centered in the Valle de Guadalupe, a small river valley nestled between the border and the beaches I grew up on. The Valle anchors Mexico's principal wine region. It's also the cradle of a new wave of culinarians, artists, architects, and dreamers who combine a passion for Mexico with an appreciation of the limitlessness of Baja's possibilities.

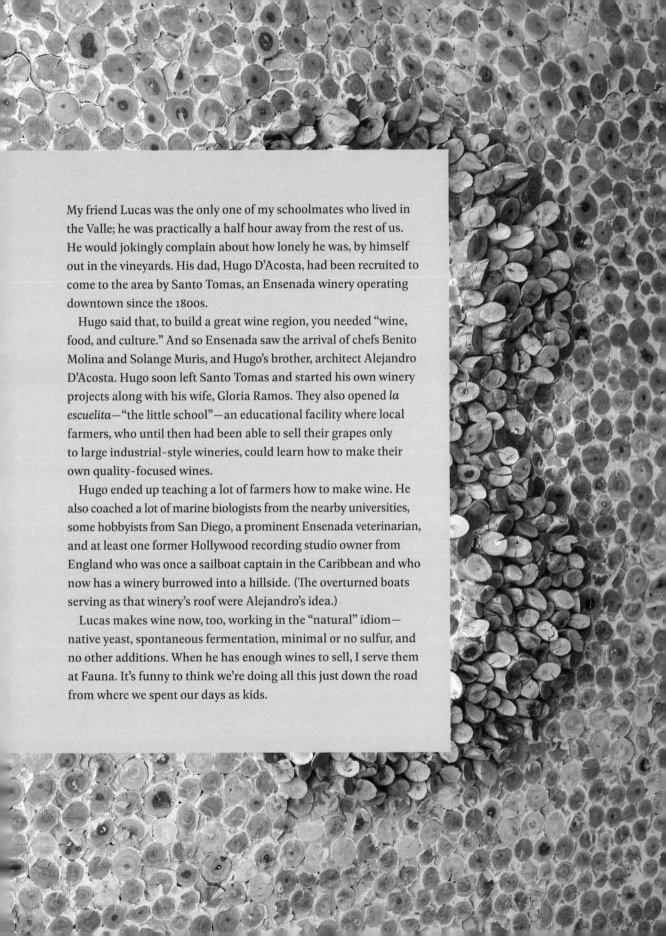

My friend Lucas was the only one of my schoolmates who lived in
the Valle; he was practically a half hour away from the rest of us.
He would jokingly complain about how lonely he was, by himself
out in the vineyards. His dad, Hugo D'Acosta, had been recruited to
come to the area by Santo Tomas, an Ensenada winery operating
downtown since the 1800s.

Hugo said that, to build a great wine region, you needed "wine,
food, and culture." And so Ensenada saw the arrival of chefs Benito
Molina and Solange Muris, and Hugo's brother, architect Alejandro
D'Acosta. Hugo soon left Santo Tomas and started his own winery
projects along with his wife, Gloria Ramos. They also opened *la
escuelita*—"the little school"—an educational facility where local
farmers, who until then had been able to sell their grapes only
to large industrial-style wineries, could learn how to make their
own quality-focused wines.

Hugo ended up teaching a lot of farmers how to make wine. He
also coached a lot of marine biologists from the nearby universities,
some hobbyists from San Diego, a prominent Ensenada veterinarian,
and at least one former Hollywood recording studio owner from
England who was once a sailboat captain in the Caribbean and who
now has a winery burrowed into a hillside. (The overturned boats
serving as that winery's roof were Alejandro's idea.)

Lucas makes wine now, too, working in the "natural" idiom—
native yeast, spontaneous fermentation, minimal or no sulfur, and
no other additions. When he has enough wines to sell, I serve them
at Fauna. It's funny to think we're doing all this just down the road
from where we spent our days as kids.

Jicama
with chile, lime, and salt

2 tablespoons ancho chile powder (or other chile powder, but not "chili powder")

1 teaspoon kosher salt

Pinch of sugar

1 jicama, peeled

Juice of 2 limes

Visitors to Baja's wine country are sometimes surprised to find that many restaurants don't set out tortilla chips and salsa for guests. When places do put out a little pre-meal snack, it's typically something fresh and vibrant, in keeping with the cuisine in general. This palate-priming jicama snack is a good example; it makes a great arrival-time finger food at a grill-out or dinner party.

Mix together the chile powder, salt, and sugar in a small bowl.

Cut the jicama into thin slices, about the size of your pinky finger, and put them on a serving plate.

Pour the lime juice over the jicama slices, then sprinkle them with the chile powder mixture. Serve immediately.

Watermelon
with olive oil and chile

¼ cup ancho chile powder
(or other chile powder,
but not "chili powder")

2 teaspoons kosher salt

1 small watermelon
(4 to 5 pounds is ideal)

¼ cup extra-virgin olive oil

6 fresh mint leaves,
coarsely chopped

As with many wine regions, in the valleys around Ensenada we produce a lot of excellent olive oil. In the summer, drizzling local olive oil over fresh-cut watermelon with powdered chile makes a delicious take on a fruit salad. Be sure the olive oil you use in this dish is really tasty—the key to the flavors of the dish is the watermelon and chile interacting with the aromatics of the oil.

Mix the chile powder and salt in a small bowl.

Dice the watermelon into pieces about ¾ inch per side, discarding the rind and the bitter outer-edge meat. Put the diced pieces in a serving bowl. Pour the olive oil over the watermelon pieces, mixing so that the oil fully coats all of them. Sprinkle in the chile powder mixture and gently toss to make sure the powder clings to the watermelon pieces and doesn't collect at the bottom of the bowl.

Garnish with the mint leaves and serve.

Not too long after Hugo D'Acosta and his compadres started working in the Valle, a totally new kind of place opened here— Restaurante Laja. Laja was founded by a chef who went to high school in Tijuana, who had cooked in New York City and the Bay Area, and who would become my mentor: Jair Téllez.

Jair sees things in many layers. At Laja, he brought together the farming climate of our California, the farm-to-table spirit of the Bay Area, and a culinary inspiration that he called his "imaginary Basque grandmother." He is also a very skilled cook in the technical sense and taught me, along with many others, the exacting requirements of making great food.

His was the first restaurant I know of in the wine valley that supplied its kitchen from its own garden on the property. Grown in our hot, wine-country weather, the powerful heat of local arugula, balanced with a little fruit and local olive oil, has become a touchstone of our terroir.

Almost twenty years have passed since Laja opened. Jair has expanded his work to include Baja-inspired restaurants in Mexico City, Cancun, and Vancouver, British Columbia, as well as a natural-wine project near us called Bichi. And his restaurant here, still as thoughtful as ever, is now just one of many in the Valle that serve salads from their own garden.

Arugula fall salad

3 figs (black or green)

1 pear

3 tablespoons pomegranate molasses

⅓ cup extra-virgin olive oil

½ teaspoon kosher salt

½ teaspoon black pepper

3 cups loosely packed arugula

8 slices aged cheese, such as Pecorino or aged Gouda

When watermelon season is over, it's time to move to this salad featuring the autumn crop of pears and figs. Pomegranate molasses, which brings in another fall flavor, is something you typically find in the international section of your grocery store, in a Middle Eastern specialty store, or online.

Stem the figs and slice them into eighths. Peel and core the pear and dice it into pieces no bigger than ½ inch per side.

Using a whisk, mix the pomegranate molasses, olive oil, salt, and pepper in a bowl.

On each plate, put a serving of arugula and fig eighths. Top each salad with the pear cubes. Pour the molasses-oil mixture over all and top with the cheese slices. Serve immediately.

ON MEXICAN CHEESE

The world of Mexican cheese is full and complex; to address it with proper depth would require a book in itself. For that reason, here we offer only a tiny discussion of a few cheeses relevant to these recipes.

Cotija is perhaps most easily understood as the Mexican equivalent to Parmesan cheese. It's dry and salty, and it crumbles into a powder that is typically applied to a dish immediately before serving. However, while it has those traits in common with its Italian cousin, Cotija is its own cheese. Cotija is fairly soft for a dry cheese, and it has a notable tanginess. It's often sprinkled on refried beans and other earthy favorites to add bright and somewhat salty notes.

Queso asadero literally translates to "grilling cheese"; it's an easy-melting cheese that originated in the north of mainland Mexico, where outdoor cooking is a way of life. Asadero's mild flavor and smooth texture make it great with seafood, particularly when melted, as in Almejas Rellenas (Loreto-Style Stuffed Clams, page 104) or Gobernador Tacos (Shrimp, Poblano, and Cheese Tacos, page 147).

Of course, townsfolk in Baja shop at Costco just like people north of border, and the products at our stores aren't that different from products in the north. What this means is that a lot of the time, even in some very down-home places, the melting cheese being used is mass-market mozzarella. Truthfully, this cheese tastes good and is really easy to work with. Don't let anyone try to tell you it's not authentic!

On the opposite end of the craft spectrum, we also have a robust and exciting universe of artisanal cheesemaking in Baja. Here in wine country, two of the most established producers are Tito Cortes and Marcelo Ramonetti.

Tito grew up in Ensenada, where his father came to work as harbormaster in the 1950s. Over time, the family's interest in livestock and cheesemaking became a vanguard for the whole region. My dad would buy his ranch cattle from Tito because of their excellent breeding; now I buy his pork to serve at the restaurant because of its excellent flavor. When the first practitioners of high-end gastronomy established themselves here, Tito invested in the production of artisanal cheeses. His cheeses are honest and delicious. They were being served at our region's best restaurants when the restaurants first opened, and they are still being served there today.

Marcelo's family moved here in 1880, from San Luis Obispo and, before that, from Switzerland. They worked in a cattle camp cooking for the workers in Real del Castillo—a now-tiny Baja mining town that in those days was the capital of the whole state. Marcelo's ranch is in that same area, and now, instead of feeding miners, he's putting world-class cheeses on the tables of the finest restaurants in Mexico.

The cheeses made by Tito and Marcelo are perfect choices for recipes such as Arugula Fall Salad (page 179). Unfortunately, at this time, there's no convenient way to legally obtain these cheeses in the United States, so you'll have to make a point to experience them when you visit us in person.

Uni breakfast sandwiches

¼ onion, peeled

1 serrano chile, stemmed

1 small tomato, stemmed

4 eggs

4 teaspoons heavy cream

1 small avocado

1 teaspoon kosher salt

2 tablespoons butter

8 tongues of uni (see page 253)

8 slices brioche bread or other light sandwich bread

We call it *erizo*, but U.S. cooks have settled on the word *uni*, borrowed from Japanese, to describe the edible part of sea urchin. Its bright, seafoam taste is uniquely refreshing, and I particularly enjoy it early in the day. Alongside things tangy and salty—such as the combination of beer, salt, and lime juice we call a *michelada*—it makes a perfect breakfast refresher on those mornings when a fun time the night before has you slow to wake up.

Dice the onion as small as you comfortably can and put it in a small bowl. Slice the serrano into thin discs and add the slices to the bowl with the onion.

Using a serrated knife, dice the tomato as small as you can without working too hard. Discard any juice and seeds that run out and set the diced portion aside.

Crack the eggs into a medium bowl. Add the cream to the eggs and mix with a fork or whisk until fully blended.

Halve the avocado, remove the pit and stem, and cut the flesh into long narrow slices (about ¼ inch thick) while it is still sitting in its skin. Sprinkle a small pinch of the salt on each side. Put the two halves together back into a hollowed-out zombie avocado, to keep the flesh from browning while it sits for a few minutes.

Warm a frying pan or griddle over medium heat. You're going to use this to crisp the bread right before serving.

In a separate saucepan, melt the butter over low heat and add the remaining salt. Keep cooking the butter until it is brown, taking care not to let it burn. Once the butter is brown, pour half of it into a small bowl and set that aside to cool a little.

Add the onion and serrano to the pan with the brown butter, turn the heat to medium, and cook for 1 minute. Add the tomato and cook for 1 minute more. Put the eggs into the pan along with 4 of the uni tongues. Cook, while scrambling the mixture, for 1 minute. Turn off the burner and cover the pan with its lid, both to keep everything in it warm and to let the eggs finish cooking.

Spread the reserved brown butter on both sides of each brioche slice.

One by one (or more at once if you have room in the pan), toast the bread in the frying pan, flipping once, so both sides are golden brown. After browning the second slice, top it with one-fourth of the egg-uni mixture. On the face of the first slice, spread one of the remaining uni tongues. Then, using a small spoon, dig into one of the avocado halves and remove one quarter of the total avocado slices, spreading them out over the bread so that as much as possible is covered. Put the first bread slice on top of the second slice to make a proper sandwich and cut along the diagonal. Repeat until all four sandwiches are prepared.

Serve immediately.

Yellowtail sashimi
(tiradito de jurel)

1 pound yellowtail fillet, sushi-grade

Juice of 4 limes

4 teaspoons soy sauce

4 teaspoons sesame oil or extra-virgin olive oil

3 tablespoons rice vinegar

½ red onion, peeled

One ½-inch piece fresh ginger

1 serrano chile, stemmed

¼ bunch fresh cilantro

Tiradito is a Peruvian dish that marries elements of Latin American ceviche with Japanese sashimi. One version of it became well-known and well-loved in Ensenada at restaurants founded by chefs Benito Molina and Solange Muris, who currently own and operate Restaurante Manzanilla on the harbor downtown. In Ensenada, this dish typically features whatever catch was landed that morning by a local fisherman, and most often that fish is *jurel* (yellowtail jack).

In making the sauce, you can use regular sesame oil or the toasted kind, depending on your preference (and what's already in your pantry). In our region, which of course is not just an international fishing port but also wine country, sometimes the sesame oil is swapped out entirely for a piquant olive oil.

The photo opposite is from the restaurant La Casita in Todos Santos, in Baja California Sur. Good sashimi is beloved on the whole peninsula!

Cut the fish into thin slices as if you are making sashimi. If you're already skilled at this, great! You can move on to preparing the vegetables and sauce and cut your sashimi according to your own method.

On the other hand, if you've never cut sashimi before, here is a method to get you started. First, make sure you have a very sharp knife. Second, wrap the fish fillet tightly in plastic wrap and shape it—using your hands outside the wrap—more or less into a cylinder. (If you're buying sushi-grade fillets of yellowtail or tuna in the United States, it will likely be a fairly cylindrical-shaped loin piece already.) Put the fish in the freezer for 30 to 60 minutes, just long enough for it to become firm without being actually frozen.

continued

In a medium bowl, combine the lime juice, soy sauce, sesame oil, and rice vinegar and mix it all together briefly with a fork or whisk. Put the bowl in the fridge.

Finely dice the onion and put it in a small bowl.

Peel the ginger. (I like to use the back edge of a spoon for this, but you also can use the back of a knife or even a vegetable peeler.) Mince the peeled ginger either in a food processor or by dicing it very finely with a knife. Add the minced ginger to the onion.

Dice the serrano as small as you can and add it to the onion-ginger mix. Then remove the thick stem bases of the cilantro and discard them. Chop the tender parts small and add them to the onion-ginger-chile mix.

Remove the fish from the freezer, peel back the first ½ inch or so of the plastic wrap, and slice off a piece of fish that is between ⅛ inch and ¼ inch thick. Working deliberately but without delay, slice the remaining fish in the same manner. If you need to stop and refreeze the fish, you can do so, but be sure to refrigerate what you've already sliced.

Arrange the fish slices in a single layer on a serving plate, nestled against one another like tiles on the bottom of a fountain. Drizzle the soy sauce mixture over the fish, covering it all equally. Sprinkle with the onion-ginger-chile mixture. Serve immediately.

Oysters
with green apple and lemon verbena

For the lemon verbena emulsion

3 tablespoons fresh-squeezed lime juice

1 pound fresh (not dried) lemon verbena

3 tablespoons neutral oil, such as canola oil

Pinch of kosher salt

½ teaspoon xanthan gum or guar gum

2 teaspoons water

6 oysters

1 green apple (a tart variety such as Granny Smith is ideal)

Pretty much every chef in Ensenada and wine country has his or her own take on oysters on the half shell. Our oysters here are really good. They make the perfect start to any leisurely meal; you can savor the flavor of the ocean and prime your palate without getting filled up. Whenever I go to a friend's restaurant, I order the oysters and think about how they're presented, just to enjoy getting on the chef's wavelength.

You can guess that at Fauna we have a distinctive version. We shuck the oysters and put the meat on thin slices of green apple. At first it looks as if they're in their shell, then you realize you can eat the whole thing. Meanwhile the apple's tart acid complements the oyster meat much like a traditional mignonette. In place of oyster liquor, we include an emulsion of lime, oil, and lemon verbena. A little xanthan gum or guar gum gives the texture needed to hold the oyster in place.

To make the lemon verbena emulsion: Put the lime juice, lemon verbena, oil, salt, xanthan gum, and water in a blender or food processor and blend until the mixture emulsifies. Sometimes this can take a little longer than you think it will, even as much as a couple minutes.

Shuck each oyster and detach the meat.

Cut two big lobes off of the green apple so that you have two half-spherical "halves" and a center wedge that includes the core. Throw the center wedge away. Cut the outside cap off each lobe, so that you are left with two hockey puck–shaped apple cross-sections. Slice each puck into paper-thin (or as thin as you can make) circles—you will need one circle for each oyster. In each circle, cut from the center to an edge. Then make a cone shape with each apple slice.

Put the meat from one oyster into each apple cone. Top with the lemon verbena emulsion. Put it in a shot glass to serve or hand it to someone to eat.

Charred cabbage
with puree and salsa negra

1 head green cabbage

1 recipe Cabbage Puree (facing page), hot

1 recipe Salsa Negra (page 56)

2 tablespoons Mexican crema, crème fraîche, or sour cream

4 teaspoons extra-virgin olive oil (or other type of salad oil, such as walnut oil)

Kosher salt

For serving

Corn tortillas (see page 142)

Here's a produce-forward dish that's particularly well suited as an appetizer at a backyard dinner party or any other outdoor cooking occasion. The char on the featured cabbage nicely picks up the smoky chiles in the salsa negra and the cabbage puree.

If you're making the dish indoors, you can blister the cabbage using the oven broiler instead of a grill.

Preheat the grill or broiler to its maximum temperature.

Cut the cabbage into quarters. Using the grill or oven broiler, char both cut sides of each quarter.

Turn the heat of the grill to medium-high or change the oven temperature to 450°F. Bake the cabbage for 7 minutes, until it is soft.

Put a spoonful of cabbage puree on each plate. Spoon some salsa negra into the center of the puree and add a generous dollop of the crema in the center of the salsa. Place the cabbage on the crema and bathe with the olive oil.

Season with salt and serve with corn tortillas.

Cabbage puree

1 pound green cabbage
(about half a head)

¾ cup butter

10 pieces dried morita chile
(smoked jalapeño), stemmed
and cut into strips

½ teaspoon kosher salt

1 tablespoon white vinegar

Morita chile is a type of dried chipotle (smoked jalapeño chile). You can find them in most places where Mexican dried chiles are sold (see page 253). If you can't find morita chile, use any other type of chipotle.

Preheat the broiler to its maximum temperature.

Cut the cabbage into wafers about ½ inch thick. Put the slices onto a sheet pan and char them under the broiler, flipping once if possible. (They will tend to fall apart; don't worry if you can't flip them.) When they are charred, remove them from the broiler.

In a sauté pan, melt the butter over low heat until it is browned and has a hazelnut aroma. Add the charred cabbage and the morita chile strips and turn the heat to medium. Sauté the cabbage and moritas in the browned butter until the cabbage is soft and integrated with the chile.

Remove the pan from the heat, let cool slightly, and then put the mixture in the bowl of a blender or food processor. Blend it until the texture is smooth and any big lumps are gone.

Add the salt and vinegar, blend for a couple more pulses, and then serve.

Pickled pork skin and grilled oyster tostadas

For the cueritos

4 jalapeño chiles

¼ cup coriander seed

½ onion, peeled and quartered

1 garlic bulb, top removed

⅓ cup kosher salt

1 pound pork skin, fat layer attached (see "Purchasing Notes," page 251)

1½ cups white vinegar

2 bay leaves

5 dried arbol chiles, stemmed

12 small or medium oysters

6 red radishes

6 tostada crisps (see page 142)

⅓ cup Salsa Negra (page 56)

In Mexico, we have two main ways of preparing pork skin—frying it into *chicharrones*, which you already know about, and pickling it, which makes *cueritos*. You can eat *cueritos* right from the jar as a tangy treat. Supermarkets sell *cueritos* in large plastic jars; they're considered a rough-and-ready snack, not what you'd expect to eat in an upscale restaurant. But they can work well in complex dishes. As with many foods, they taste better when they're handmade. This recipe is for the grill because that's the easiest way to cook oysters.

To make the *cueritos*: Fill a stockpot with water and add the jalapeños, 2 tablespoons of the coriander seed, the onion, garlic, and salt. Bring the water to a boil and add the pork skin. Turn the heat to a low boil and cook for 1 hour and 45 minutes.

Heat the vinegar in a small saucepan at a simmer.

Remove the pork skin from the stockpot and put it in a bowl or large mason jar. Fill the jar with the vinegar. Add the bay leaves, arbol chiles, and remaining 2 tablespoons coriander seed. Let sit for at least 1 hour, or refrigerate and eat within 1 week.

Preheat the grill to medium. Put the oysters on the grill and cook with the grill lid closed, checking them periodically. Remove each oyster when its shell pops open (typically between 15 and 30 minutes). If any oyster shells resist opening, discard them.

As the oysters cook, cut the *cueritos* into rectangular pieces resembling the tip of your finger, about 1 inch long by ⅓ inch wide.

Slice the radishes into discs about ⅛ inch thick. Lay out the tostada crisps. Coat each with a thin layer of salsa negra, then add the radish slices and the *cueritos* pieces.

When the oysters have cooled enough to touch, use an oyster knife or regular knife to remove the meat, and plop it on the *cueritos*, 2 oysters per tostada. Serve immediately.

Abalone in green sauce

4 ounces abalone, trimmed, or a meaty white fish such as halibut, cut into thin 3-inch-long pieces

All-purpose flour for dusting, plus 1 tablespoon

4 cups neutral frying oil

½ cup panko crumbs (or crushed chicharrones, see page 114)

1 egg

¼ cup extra-virgin olive oil

2 tablespoons chopped white onion

2 tablespoons Tomatillo/Avocado Sauce (page 78)

1⅓ cups fine-chopped spinach

2 teaspoons sour cream

It wasn't long ago that wild abalone was abundant in both Californias, but, as they take many years to grow to maturity, they were very susceptible to overfishing. The populations were eventually devastated, particularly in Southern California on the U.S. side, and for their protection, it's no longer legal to buy wild-harvested abalone in U.S. California. However, a few abalone farms have arisen to meet the demand for what is a precious, delicate, and delicious ingredient.

It's really easy to cook up a tasty abalone meal. If you happen to find yourself with some abalone and about five minutes to spare, just sauté them in butter, add onions and garlic, and then quickly deglaze the pan with broth. Instant appetizer!

In California—when time allows—abalone is traditionally dusted with bread crumbs or panko before being pan-fried. In the recipe we present here, we use the panko but then go for a full deep-fry, inspired by the street cooking you see throughout Baja. Also in the Baja spirit, feel free to substitute crushed *chicharrones* for the panko.

Pat down the abalone with paper towels to dry it out a little. Put a bit of flour in a dish. Lightly dust each side of the abalone with flour. This will help dry out the abalone a little more. Cover the abalone and put it back in the fridge for 5 to 10 minutes, just until lightly chilled.

In a wok or Dutch oven, heat the frying oil to 365°F. While the oil is heating, use a fork or your hands to mix the panko and remaining 1 tablespoon flour in a bowl. Put the egg in a separate bowl and whip it until the yolk and white are blended and a little bit fluffy.

Retrieve the abalone from the fridge. Briefly dip the abalone in the egg and let the excess run off. Then dredge the abalone in the panko mixture until it is fully covered with crumbs.

continued

Abalone in green sauce, continued

Line a plate with paper towels. When the frying oil is heated, working in batches if necessary, and without crowding the pan, add the abalone and deep-fry for 1 minute, or until the breading is medium-brown. Place on the paper towel–lined plate and pat down to wick away excess oil.

In a medium saucepan, warm the olive oil over medium heat. Add the onion and cook until it becomes aromatic (2 to 3 minutes) and then add the tomatillo/avocado sauce, spinach, and sour cream. Stir for 40 seconds, just until the spinach is wilted and the sauce is blended.

Place the abalone on a plate, pour the sauce alongside it, and serve.

Octopus and domingo rojo beans

½ pound Domingo rojo beans or other white beans such as navy beans, cooked (see page 51)

3½ ounces radishes

½ pint cherry tomatoes

4 teaspoons malt vinegar

4 teaspoons red wine vinegar

2 teaspoons extra-virgin olive oil

Kosher salt or finishing salt

12 ounces Basic Octopus (page 119)

1 tablespoon neutral cooking oil, such as canola oil

2 ounces chicharrones (see page 114), broken into 1-inch-long pieces

Cilantro, chopped, for garnish (optional)

This is an easy-to-make dish that shows off many elements of contemporary Baja cooking: fresh produce, crisp flavors, and crunchy umami complementing delicious seafood. If you're cooking outdoors, you can prepare everything but the octopus ahead of time and then finish the octopus on the grill.

Note: Delfino cilantro, which is milder, is nice for this dish, but regular cilantro works great, too.

Pull the beans from the fridge an hour or two before serving so they come to room temperature.

When ready to serve, chop the radishes and tomatoes into medium-size pieces. Mix them with the beans in a serving bowl. Add both vinegars and the olive oil, and season with salt.

Cut the octopus into pieces between 1 and 3 inches long. Warm the cooking oil in a sauté pan over high heat. Add the octopus pieces and sear them until their outsides are slightly crispy, 4 to 8 minutes per side depending on thickness. (Alternatively, you can cook them on a grill over high heat, brushed with a little olive oil, until they have darkened, crisped edges.)

Transfer the octopus to the bowl with the vegetables and beans. Mix it all together with your hands or salad tongs. Top with the *chicharrones* and cilantro, if desired, and serve.

Charred octopus in citrus-soy sauce

2 limes

½ pound Basic Octopus
(page 119)

1 tablespoon neutral cooking
oil, such as canola oil

½ cup unsalted roasted
peanuts

⅓ cup butter

½ onion, peeled and
diced small

1 garlic clove, peeled and
minced

5 dried arbol chiles, stemmed

1 cup chicharrones
(see page 114), broken
into ½-inch pieces

2 tablespoons soy sauce

½ teaspoon kosher salt

Octopus and *chicharrones* go very well together. The pork skins'
crunch complements the octopus's softness, while their flavors are
mild yet diverse. This dish takes that combo and adds nuttiness and
spice from peanuts and arbol chiles. It also adds the acid and Asian
inflection of citrus and soy sauce. The recipe is inspired by one of many
delightful dishes at Finca Altozano, a festive wine-country *asadero*
(outdoor kitchen) helmed by our friend Chef Javier Plascencia.

You'll find this an easy "small plate" for any gathering; scale it as
needed, searing the octopus in batches.

Zest the limes and then juice them. Set aside the zest and juice
in separate bowls.

Cut the octopus into pieces less than 1 inch on any side.

Warm the cooking oil in a frying pan over high heat. Add the octopus
and sear the pieces until browned, 2 to 4 minutes per side. Remove
the pieces and set aside, letting them cool to room temperature.

In a dry saucepan over medium heat, toast the peanuts until they
brown, stirring continuously so they don't blacken, 8 to 10 minutes.
Set aside.

Melt 1 teaspoon of the butter in a second frying pan over medium
heat, taking care not to burn the butter. Add the onion and cook for
5 minutes. Add the garlic and cook for 2 minutes, stirring and adding
a little water as needed to keep everything from drying out. Add the
chiles and cook for another 2 minutes. Then add the peanuts and
cook for 2 minutes more.

Turn the heat to low and add ½ cup of the *chicharrones*, the octopus,
soy sauce, and lime juice. Stir to ensure the ingredients are fully mixed
and heated. Add the remaining butter and the salt. Keep stirring until
the butter is melted.

Spoon the octopus mixture onto a deep plate and finish with the
remaining ½ cup *chicharrones* and the lime zest. Serve immediately.

Duck carnitas
with mussels and crostini

For the carnitas

1 pound duck fat (see "Purchasing Notes," page 251) or other cooking fat or cooking oil

12 ounces Honey-Roasted Duck (page 72)

1 garlic clove, peeled and minced

½ bunch parsley, minced

Juice of 4 limes

1 teaspoon kosher salt

½ cup extra-virgin olive oil, plus 1 tablespoon

1 tablespoon butter

½ pound mussels

½ cup white wine

1 baguette

In Baja, we're pretty free with mixing meat and seafood. I'm not sure if this recipe is best described as duck with mussels or mussels with duck, but they are delicious together no matter the order. The white wine and butter mix with the carnitas' *jus*; sop it all up with crisped baguette slices. Or use flour tortillas (see page 38) if you've just made some!

To make the carnitas: Melt the duck fat in a pot or Dutch oven over medium-low heat. Add the duck meat. Cook for 1 hour, keeping the heat at medium-low so that the fat doesn't start to smoke. After an hour, the duck meat should be a little dry and somewhat crispy. Remove from the heat and set aside.

Preheat the oven to 350°F.

Mix the garlic, parsley, lime juice, salt, and ½ cup olive oil in a big bowl.

Melt the butter in a large, deep pan over medium heat, making sure the butter doesn't burn. Once the butter is hot, add the mussels to the pan and then pour the olive oil mixture over them. After 30 seconds, add the white wine. Let the mussels bathe in the liquid and steam as they cook, until they open, which could take anywhere from 4 to 15 minutes. If you have sufficient room to cover the pan, that will make the cooking go faster. When each mussel is done cooking, it will open. If any mussel refuses to open, discard that mussel–it's gone bad.

While the mussels are cooking, cut the baguette into 12 slices. Drizzle ¼ teaspoon olive oil on one side of each piece and place the pieces on a sheet tray, oiled-side up. Put the slices in the oven for 3 minutes.

When the mussels are done cooking, remove their top shells and arrange them on a serving plate. Spoon the cooking liquid generously into each mussel and follow that with a big portion of the duck carnitas. Surround with the crostini and serve.

Duck in demi-glace
with eggplant puree

For the demi-glaze

1 duck carcass (left over from Honey-Roasted Duck, page 72)

17½ cups water

For the eggplant puree

1 small eggplant (about 1½ pounds)

⅓ cup butter

1 onion, peeled, and sliced or coarsely chopped

1 cup malt vinegar

½ cup heavy cream

4 grams squid ink or cuttlefish ink

Pinch of xanthan gum (or guar gum)

Kosher salt

Pulled meat from 2 ducks (see page 72)

Your choice of salsa (optional)

It can be hard for a cook of any cuisine to make a complete-feeling dish that doesn't have any flour or other grains. But given how a lot of people like to eat, it's nice to have something like that at your fingertips. In this recipe, we use an eggplant puree in the place where you might typically find potatoes or polenta. The key to getting the texture of the puree right is to use a little bit of thickener. Xanthan gum or guar gum are a couple dependable choices, though if you are practiced with arrowroot or cornstarch, you'll be able to make those work here, too.

To make the demi-glace: Boil the duck carcass in a stockpot with 16 cups of the water until reduced to about 1½ cups of liquid; this should take a few hours. Add the remaining 1½ cups water and continue boiling until there is about ½ cup of liquid left in the pot. Remove from the heat. Discard the duck carcass and let the liquid cool.

To make the eggplant puree: Remove the eggplant ends and slice the eggplant in half lengthwise. On a very hot grill or under the broiler, cook the eggplant halves face-to-the-flame until they are well charred. Remove from the heat and set aside.

Melt the butter in a large pot over medium heat. Add the onion and let it cook for about 5 minutes, until it softens and changes color. Add the charred eggplant halves and cook for 7 minutes, stirring if needed to keep them from sticking to the pan and burning. Add the malt vinegar. Let the mixture continue to cook until there is about as much liquid in the pot as there was before you added the vinegar. Expect this to take 10 to 15 minutes.

Remove the pot from the heat and let it cool for only 2 minutes. Then put all the contents of the pot in a blender, along with the cream. Puree to a smooth liquid consistency. Add the squid ink and xanthan gum and puree a little more; the mixture should thicken to the point where it is not runny.

continued

Duck in demi-glace, continued

Sample the mixture and season with salt, blending a little more once the salt is added.

Rewarm the pulled duck in a pan over medium heat. (Use a little oil or water in the pan if you need it to keep the duck from sticking.) If the demi-glace has fully cooled, warm it up over low heat, but don't let it get too hot to eat.

On each plate or shallow bowl, spoon some of the eggplant puree. Put a portion of duck alongside it. Pour the demi-glace in between the duck and the puree. Top the duck with salsa if desired. Serve immediately.

Duck tamal in black chipotle sauce

---

8 corn husks (see "Purchasing Notes," page 251), plus more as needed

2 cups neutral cooking oil, such as canola oil

3 ounces dried *chipotle meco* (aka *chipotle seco*)

1 tablespoon kosher salt, plus 1 teaspoon

1 tablespoon sugar

14 ounces corn masa (see page 142)

4 ounces duck fat

1 teaspoon baking soda

1 pound Honey-Roasted Duck (page 72)

For serving

2 cups refried black beans (see page 32)

Tamales are a well-known Christmastime tradition in both Californias, but on the Mexican side of the border, we eat them the rest of the year as well. In Baja, where we particularly enjoy small game, duck makes an elegant *tamal* filling.

Detailed instructions for shaping the tamales are included in this recipe (there is no need to tie as pictured on the next page). Once you know how to do this, you can make tamales with almost any filling, as long as the filling is somewhat stewy.

Tamales freeze very well and can be reheated directly from the freezer using either steam (in a steamer or Dutch oven) or a microwave.

This recipe's sauce calls for dried chipotle chiles (called either *chipotle seco* or *chipotle meco*), which are becoming easier to find in U.S. markets these days. Suggestions for how to find different types of dried chiles are on page 253. However, if you can't locate dried chipotles, you can substitute canned chipotles. Canned chiles will fry more quickly than dried chiles, so just adjust the frying time accordingly.

One hour before starting, put the corn husks in a bowl or pot full of water, with a plate on top to keep them submerged. If you can soak them for several hours before starting, even better. You want them to develop a flexible consistency where you can trust them not to break if manhandled.

Heat the cooking oil to 375°F in a large pot or Dutch oven. Add the chiles, grouping them in medium-size batches so the oil doesn't come down in temperature for more than a minute or so, and fry until they have reinflated and look a little moist; this will take a few minutes. When the chiles are puffed up, remove them and put them in a bowl. When you are done frying all the chiles, turn off the burner and set the oil aside.

continued

Duck tamal in black chipotle sauce, continued

Once the oil has cooled enough to handle, put 1 tablespoon of the oil into the bowl of a blender or food processor, along with the chiles, 1 tablespoon salt, and the sugar. Blend into a smooth liquid. When blending, keeping adding the used cooking oil as necessary to make the sauce a rich liquid. If you have to blend in batches because your blender is too small to handle all the contents, that's fine; just mix the batches together in a bowl when you're done. Set the sauce aside.

In a large bowl, mix the masa with the duck fat and baking soda. Add the remaining 1 teaspoon salt and knead until the dough no longer sticks in your hands.

Put the duck meat in a dry frying pan over medium heat, letting some fat render out while the duck is heating. Stir as necessary to make sure all the duck gets browned and doesn't stick to the pan.

Remove from the heat and put the meat in a bowl with the black chipotle sauce. Toss the duck in the sauce so the meat is fully coated.

Remove the corn husks from their soaking container and shake off any excess water, using a paper towel to dry each one if necessary. Spread out one corn husk. One side of the corn husk is a little smoother than the other; it's easier to work with if you have this smooth side facing up, but it's not a crisis if you forget. You'll need a minimum width of 6 inches, so if the corn husk is narrower than that, make a bigger husk surface by overlapping a second corn husk, oriented in the same direction (wide end of each husk on the same side).

Working from the wide end of the corn husk (as opposed to the pointy or narrow end), use a knife to spread a layer of masa starting at the end to about halfway down the husk, about 4 inches wide, with the left edge of the masa running along the left edge of the corn husk. The masa should be about as thick as you would spread

continued

peanut butter in making a sandwich (at least ⅛ inch thick). Repeat with the remaining corn husks and end the process with eight laid out in front of you.

In the center of each corn husk's masa cushion, put an equal portion of the duck meat. Add sauce if needed to fully cover the duck meat, but try keep the amount of sauce low enough that it doesn't run out off the edge of the masa—excess sauce may create dark splotches that show through the skin of the finished tamal. Be sure to leave 1 inch of untopped masa at the end of the husk (the wide end where the masa is).

Once the filling is in place, roll the tamal along the axis defined by the ribs of the corn husk. To do this, place the left edge of the corn husk (the edge that has masa right up to it with no margin) close to you. Then fold it away from you, over the filling, to a place where the masa on the lip of the near edge meets the masa on the far edge of the masa cushion. There should be a couple inches of corn husk without masa beyond this point; the shape should now be like the letter *P* lying on its back, with your hands over the half circle. In your hands, you now have a corn dog–shaped roll with stuffing inside it. Using your fingertips, squeeze the roll into more of a cylindrical shape, fusing the masa joint together. Then, using your right hand, fold the un-masa'd, narrow side of the husk over the corn dog part. This is the first part of tucking in the end. Now, slowly roll the corn dog part away from you until you have something between a cylinder and a cone. It should be open at one end and closed at the other, with the tail tucked into the roll.

Next, you should be able to close the top of the tamal by gently squeezing the lip flat in the direction it already tends to want to be flat. The masa on that end, which you did not cover with filling, will fuse to itself on both sides, making a nice seal. It's not essential that the tamales be sealed, but it helps make sure no filling gets out when you cook them.

Place the tamales in a steamer or on a roasting rack in a Dutch oven with water beneath and steam until they give off a heady, corn-tortilla aroma, 30 to 75 minutes. Typically they need about 15 minutes more after that point. You can check and see if they are done by peeling the husk back on one—being careful not to burn yourself with the steam—and making sure the masa is cooked firm and supple but not overcooked and dry.

Serve each tamal on a plate with a scoop of refried beans. Every diner can unwrap the tamal on his or her plate before devouring it.

A quarter-mile off the main highway in the valley, under a sprawling pine tree, chef Ismene Venegas cooks at her outdoor restaurant, El Pinar de 3 Mujeres. Although a few years my senior, she's in the new generation of chefs. Like me, she grew up here, and she worked in the kitchen at Laja and also for Baja chefs in Mexico City. She helmed a restaurant in downtown Ensenada for a few years before moving to this location, outside the winery where her mom is a partner and winemaker.

When Ismene is not cooking, she walks the canyons and mesas, communing with the plants of the chaparral. She forages mostly in the winter, the rainy season here, when the restaurant is quieter and rattlesnakes aren't afoot. In those cooler weeks, the plants exude their vitality, in contrast to the hot and dry summer, when most do little more than survive.

Sage, which she cultivates in her restaurant garden, is a staple in Ismene's kitchen. She infuses white sage (*Salvia apiana*) into butter or olive oil and then uses the flavored fat for baking desserts, like almond biscuits. Black sage (*Salvia mellifera*) leaves are subtly and delicately mixed into salads. Coastal sage (*Salvia munzii*) is dehydrated, crushed, and mixed into a pot of cooked beans, inspired by the similar use in Oaxaca of avocado leaves.

As kids, we are taught not to eat the little red berries from our native holly, toyon (*Heteromeles arbutifolia*), because they'll upset our stomachs. But, as with elderberries, when they are dried, crushed, and cooked, they are edible and have a distinct, delicious flavor. Ismene uses the syrup as a cooking liquid for sous vide. She infuses yerba santa (*Eriodictyon sessilifolium*), a very common medicinal plant here, into milk or other liquids for cooking.

I think the work Ismene is doing both in research—she just coauthored a book on cooking with our native plants—and at her restaurant holds a lot of potential for our shared culinary future. Modern Baja cooking has developed into its current state by incorporating contributions of many generations. It may be that, among the next ideas to be widely adopted, we'll see a deeper use of these ingredients that have been here much longer than we have.

Campfire quail
with piñon sauce

For the piñon sauce

1 tomato

2 garlic cloves, peeled

¼ onion, peeled

1 corn tortilla (see page 142)

1 ancho chile (dried poblano),
top removed

1 dried pasilla chile

2 dried chipotle chiles

3 dried cascabel chiles

½ teaspoon whole cloves

½ teaspoon black pepper

½ teaspoon ground cumin

⅓ cup pine nuts

½ cup neutral cooking oil,
such as canola oil

4 cups water, plus more
as needed

4 ounces *piloncillo* sugar,
plus more as needed

¼ cup unsweetened
cocoa powder

3 tablespoons brown sugar

Kosher salt

For the quail

4 cups water

⅓ cup kosher salt

6 quail

½ cup extra-virgin olive oil

For serving

Mexican White Rice (page 220)

continued

In modern Baja cuisine, perhaps the longest-established signature is cooking with small game. One of the early "new wave" Baja chefs, Miguel Angel Guerrero, is an avid hunter and has encouraged many other contemporary chefs to work freely with the rabbits, ducks, and quail that had already long been an important part of the area's food culture. Wood-fired quail is something you encounter quite often in Valle restaurants, both in rustic places and high-end kitchens.

In this recipe, we serve the quail with a *piñon* (pine nut) sauce. Pine nuts, like quail, are native to the area, and I like to think that they would have been always eaten together. The *piñon* sauce calls for *piloncillo* sugar, a type of unrefined sugar that we often use in Mexican cooking. It comes in a truncated cone that is light brown in color, and typically, you hand grate it before using. You can find it in any Mexican market and often in mainstream markets as well.

This recipe, where you cook the quail in a live fire, is meant to be something you can do on a camping trip, on the beach, or in your backyard if your backyard has a fire pit. It's also fine to use a gas grill or even an oven; there's no special technique involved. Note that unless your camping setup is exceptionally well equipped, you'll have to pre-make the *piñon* sauce and rice and bring them with you.

For holding the quail in the fire, it's easiest to use a grill basket with a handle. This way you can make sure to apply the fire equally to all the sides of the bird. If you don't have a grill basket like this, you can also use a long set of tongs, a skewer, or a meat hook with an insulated handle. In a pinch, just use a cast-iron pan and an oven mitt.

Note: You might want to consider buying a grill basket with a handle; they work great for fish and many other meats.

To make the *piñon* sauce: Using either a gas grill or a sheet pan and your broiler, fully char the tomato, garlic, onion, tortilla, and all the chiles. You want the produce to be as blackened as you can get it without drying out. Remove from the heat and set them aside.

Preheat the oven to 350°F.

Put the cloves, pepper, and cumin in a small, dry saucepan over medium heat for just a minute or two, toasting them lightly until their aromatics are released.

Put the pine nuts onto a dry sheet pan and bake them for 8 minutes in the preheated oven, until they become golden.

Heat the cooking oil in large pot over high heat. Add the onion, garlic, and tomato and cook for 1 minute.

Add the spices, tortilla, and pine nuts to the pot. Stir constantly for a couple minutes and then add the charred chiles. Let cook for 2 to 3 minutes more, continuing to stir. Add the water, *piloncillo*, cocoa powder, and brown sugar. Let it cook at a simmer, uncovered, for 2 hours. If the water gets so low that it looks as if it might dry out, top it off with more water. You want about 3 cups of liquid in the pot after 2 hours.

When 2 hours have passed, put all the contents of the pot into the bowl of a blender or food processor. Blend the mixture into a liquid. Put the blended liquid in a new pot and cook for 1 hour at a simmer. Season with salt, and, if desired, season with more *piloncillo* sugar. Set aside or refrigerate for coating the quail prior to serving.

To make the quail: Mix the water and salt in a pot or deep pan. Put the quail in the saltwater solution to brine for 15 minutes.

Start your wood cooking fire. If you don't have a wood cooking fire, you can use a gas grill or the oven.

Remove the quail from the brine and brush them with the olive oil.

Put the quail in grill baskets, or attach them to skewers, and roast them in the fire. If you like your cooked meat crispy, hold the birds closer to the flame; if you prefer a more even, slower cook, hold them a little farther out, where the heat is even.

To measure their progress, pull a bird from the fire and press on it; when it feels like the inside of your palm, it's probably done. Also, if a quail is releasing clear juices, that's a sign that it's cooked. The whole cooking process typically takes 15 to 20 minutes, but the exact time will depend on the heat of your fire and how close you hold the birds to the flame. Remove the birds from the fire and let cool for a few minutes.

Reheat the pine nut sauce, if necessary.

Once the quail have come down in temperature enough so that you can easily handle them, use a paring knife to detach the legs and breast.

Dip each piece of quail in the pine nut sauce, and place them on a bed of rice. Top with any remaining pine nut sauce and serve.

Mexican white rice

---

4 teaspoons neutral cooking oil, such as canola oil

¼ onion, peeled and minced

1 garlic clove, peeled and minced

1 cup white rice (either long-grain or short-grain is good; both are used for this dish in Mexico)

2 cups water

½ teaspoon kosher salt

While Mexican restaurants in the United States mostly serve Spanish-style rice, in Mexico we often eat our rice white, with the addition of garlic and onion. Here's a simple recipe that feels like home to me.

In a pot over medium heat, warm the oil. Add the onion and garlic and cook, stirring as needed to keep them from sticking to the pan, until the onion is translucent, about 5 minutes.

Add the rice to the pot and keep stirring as needed so nothing burns. Cook until the rice is lightly browned, about 5 minutes more. Add the water and salt. Increase the heat and bring to a boil.

Once the water is at a boil, cover the pot and turn the heat to low. After 15 minutes, turn off the heat and wait for 5 minutes more. The rice should be fluffy with no water left in the pot. Serve and enjoy!

Lamb ravioli in jus

For the pasta

4 cups all-purpose flour, plus more as needed

1 teaspoon kosher salt

6 eggs

3 tablespoons extra-virgin olive oil

¼ cup water, plus more as needed

For the filling

4 cups neutral cooking oil, such as canola oil

2 ounces dried chile negro

¼ cup water, or as needed

1 teaspoon kosher salt

1 teaspoon sugar

1 pound Braised Lamb, Ranch-Style (page 24)

½ cup Mexican crema or sour cream

2 cups lamb, duck or veal broth

1 egg

½ cup kosher salt

continued

When I worked at Laja, the original "destination" restaurant in the Valle de Guadalupe, it was the first time I'd ever cooked in a kitchen of that caliber. When you go to Laja, you know you're going to get unfussy, thoughtful food made from what's local. There will be a soup and a salad from the garden, very fresh local seafood, and a bit of meat. And in the middle of the meal, almost always, you will be served a beautiful, handmade pasta dish. Sometimes it's a ravioli filled with braised meat.

This recipe, a lamb ravioli, is inspired by those pasta courses. I think this kind of simple, elegant cooking showcases the beauty of life and food in the Valle.

To make the pasta: Mix together the flour and salt in a bowl. On a clean, large work area, make a volcano shape with the flour–salt mixture. The center divot of the volcano should be about 4 inches in diameter.

Crack the eggs into the center volcano divot and gently pour the olive oil on top of them. Using a fork, start beating the eggs as they sit in the bowl created by the flour. As they circulate, the eggs will tend to grab on to the flour around them, making a wider and wider circle of the egg-oil-flour mixture. Slowly pour the water into the center of this circle as you work it. During this process, it's okay to repeatedly reset the volcano as needed, using your hands, to keep everything in a workable size. Once the eggs and water have been mostly absorbed into the flour, switch to working the dough by hand.

Squeeze the dough toward yourself, fold it over away from yourself, push down on the top of it, and then rotate it 90 degrees on the work surface. Repeat that motion over and over again, periodically giving it an extra stretch, and adding a touch of flour or water if it gets too thin or too thick to work with. When you have fully kneaded the dough, it will be smooth, it won't stick to your hands, and it will stretch nicely without breaking.

Set the dough aside and let it rest, covered, for about 45 minutes.

When the dough is done resting, make yourself a clean work area, lightly floured. Using a pasta roller, roll the dough thin, as thin as you can without breaking it. Using a knife, cut the pasta sheet into 3-inch squares. Don't be afraid to generously flour the dough sheets if you are having trouble with the dough sticking to you or to the table.

To make the filling: Warm the oil in a saucepan over medium heat. Make sure it's not so hot that it is smoking. Fry the chiles in the saucepan until they are puffy and a little soft; this will probably take about 10 minutes. Remove the pan from the heat. Once the chiles and oil cool to a workable temperature stem the chiles. Then put the chiles, water, salt, and sugar in a blender or food processor along with about 1 tablespoon of the cooking oil. Blend completely into a sauce. You may need to add additional water to thin it enough to pour; that's fine.

In a large saucepan or pot, warm the lamb meat for about 3 minutes over medium heat. Add the crema and the chile sauce from the blender. Stir until the ingredients are evenly mixed. Add 1 tablespoon of the broth, just enough to make sure everything is juicy. Continue stirring and, if needed, add broth until the mixture is pliable and easy to work with but not runny.

Remove the lamb meat pot from heat and set it aside.

Break the egg into a bowl and use a whisk to beat it into a fluffy consistency. Set aside.

Put 1 tablespoon of the sauced meat on the center of a pasta square. Be careful not to put in so much filling that the sauce runs to the edges; if that happens it will be difficult to affix the top piece. Just put a little button of moist meat and no excess liquid.

Once the filling is in place, use your finger or a tiny spoon to apply beaten egg to the perimeter of the square. Take another pasta square and place it exactly on top of the first pasta square, trapping the filling in between them. Use your fingers to gently press and then pinch the outer frame until the seam is almost invisible, sealing the ravioli. Once the ravioli is sealed, dust both sides of it with flour so that the dough won't stick when you want to move it into the cooking pot. Repeat this assembly process with each ravioli.

Fill a large stockpot with water and the salt. Bring to a rolling boil. Add the ravioli and cook for 6 to 8 minutes.

While the pasta cooks, warm the remaining broth in a small saucepan over medium heat. Bring it to just below a simmer.

When the ravioli are done cooking, remove the pot from the heat and drain the ravioli.

Divide the ravioli into equal portions and put each portion on a plate with at least ¼ inch depth (or use a bowl, if you don't have a deep enough plate). Pour an equal portion of the broth over each plate's ravioli, making a pool with the ravioli in the middle. Serve immediately.

I've known Maribel's family my whole life; her dad was our dog's veterinarian. He was a popular vet because he was good and his prices were affordable; plus, he surfed, which meant he was easygoing. And his office was located right downtown. But Maribel and I didn't really know each other because we went to different schools. We were totally different, actually. Then, when we were older, one of my best friends started dating her sister. And then the next thing you know, we were together—and have been ever since.

I'm a chef and she's a baker, and while we both work in the kitchen, what we do is pretty different. When we were coming up in our careers, we sometimes worked at the same restaurant, but most often we were at different restaurants. Over time, she gravitated to places that had some of the best dessert and baking programs in both New York and San Francisco. Even when we worked in the United States, though, we both brought our heritage as Mexicans from Baja to our cooking. Although I think her style is a lot different from mine, the way our food works together on the menu at Fauna feels just right.

I asked her to share a couple dessert recipes for this book, and here they are. In keeping with the style of the rest of the recipes we've presented, these are basically stovetop dishes. If you want to get into hard-core baking stuff, you'll have to wait for *her* book!

Serves 6

Honey semifreddo
with raw-milk ice cream and caramel crunch

For the semifreddo

1 egg, plus 4 egg yolks

⅓ cup honey

1⅓ cups heavy cream

For the caramel crunch

½ cup sugar

5 tablespoons water

4 teaspoons honey

1 tablespoon butter

1 teaspoon kosher salt

½ teaspoon baking soda

For the raw-milk
ice cream

9 cups raw milk

⅝ cup heavy cream

2½ cups powdered milk

¼ cup sugar

1 tablespoon glucose powder

½ teaspoon kosher salt

2 teaspoons xanthan gum

continued

For this dish, you need an ice-cream machine. Nowadays, electric ice-cream makers are pretty widely available for home kitchens. You can also use a wood ice-cream bucket and salted ice, but that is very old-school and a lot of work.

We make the ice cream with raw (unpasteurized) milk from a local farmer, which is why we call for it in the recipe. However that can be hard to find in parts of the United States. Feel free to substitute regular supermarket milk; the recipe will still work very well.

To make the semifreddo: Put 2 to 3 inches of water in a Dutch oven and bring to a boil.

Crack the egg into a metal mixing bowl that is wider than the Dutch oven. Add the egg yolks and honey.

Put the mixing bowl on the Dutch oven so there is an air gap of 1 to 2 inches between the top of the water and the bottom of bowl, but the bowl is being still being heated by the water. This is basically a larger, improvised double boiler; it allows you to slowly heat the mixture while making sure the bottom of the bowl doesn't get very hot.

Using a whisk, mix the eggs and honey continuously while the mixture heats. Once it reaches 165°F on an instant-read thermometer, remove from the heat and let it cool.

In a separate bowl, whip the cream using a whisk until the cream is fluffy. Then, using a spatula, add the egg mixture and gently fold it all together until everything is evenly mixed.

Put the mixture into a rectangular container, like a loaf pan, and put that in the freezer.

To make the caramel crunch: Line a baking sheet with a silicone baking mat (Silpat) and have ready another silicone mat.

Put the sugar, water, and honey in a small pot and warm over medium heat, bringing the mixture to a steady 300°F on an instant-read thermometer. Hold at 300°F until the mixture is a warm amber color, about 10 minutes. Add the butter and mix. When the temperature returns to 300°F, add the salt and baking soda and stir. When the salt and baking soda have dissolved, remove the syrup from the heat and distribute it evenly onto the prepared baking sheet.

Put the other silicone mat on top of the caramel mixture. Use a roller to press the top mat down and create an even wafer between the two mats.

Let cool to room temperature, at which point the wafer should have a crunchy texture.

To make the ice cream: Warm the raw milk and cream in a pot over medium heat. Once the mixture is warm, add the powdered milk, sugar, and glucose powder. Stir with a whisk until dissolved. Add the salt and stir again.

Continuing to stir constantly, add the xanthan gum little by little. Once the xanthan gum is fully dissolved into the mixture, pour the whole thing into a blender or food processor and blend for 20 seconds. Then put it in the fridge to cool. When the mixture is cool, put it in your ice-cream machine and freeze according to the manufacturer's instructions.

Put six deep plates in the freezer until they are cold and then remove. Slice the semifreddo into twelve pieces and put two pieces on the bottom of each plate. Crack the caramel crunch and sprinkle all over each plate. Top each plate with two scoops of the ice cream. Serve immediately.

Churros
with pumpkin ice cream and candied pumpkin

For the pumpkin ice cream

¼ cup granulated sugar

1 tablespoon glucose powder

9 cups whole milk

⅝ cup heavy cream

⅝ cup powdered milk

½ teaspoon pumpkin pie spice

1 cup pumpkin puree

½ teaspoon salt

For the candied pumpkin

4 teaspoons cal (culinary lime)

4 cups warm water, plus 2 cups cool water

2 pounds fresh pumpkin meat, cut into pieces 1 to 3 inches per side

One 8-ounce cone *piloncillo* sugar

1 cinnamon stick

1 star anise

Candied pumpkin is a deeply traditional Mexican dessert, and churros are a very popular street food, particularly at the border. This dessert brings them both together, along with an easy pumpkin ice cream. You can use any winter squash with this recipe; it doesn't have to be the same kind of pumpkins you use to make jack-o'-lanterns. But it can be!

You will need an ice-cream maker for this recipe, as well as a pastry bag (preferably with a star tip) to make the churros.

Note: It's best to offer these on deep dessert plates or in dessert bowls. You may want to prepare the plates by putting them in the freezer for an hour or so before serving.

To make the ice cream: Mix the granulated sugar and glucose in a bowl with a fork or spoon.

In a medium pot, warm the whole milk and cream over medium-low heat. Add the sugar-glucose mixture and stir. Then, while continuing to stir, add the powdered milk, pumpkin pie spice, pumpkin puree, and salt, in that order.

Once it is all warm and the powders and salt have dissolved, put the mixture in your blender or food processor and blend it thoroughly. Then put it in the fridge for an hour or two to cool.

When the mixture is cold, put it in your ice-cream maker and freeze according to the manufacturer's instructions.

To make the candied pumpkin: In a large bowl or a pot, dissolve the cal into the warm water, mixing with a wooden spoon as needed. Add the pumpkin pieces and let them soak for 1 hour.

Put the cool water into a large stockpot and add the *piloncillo*, cinnamon stick, and star anise. Bring the water to a boil. Lower the heat to a simmer and cook, stirring as needed, until the *piloncillo* has fully dissolved.

continued

Churros, continued

For the churros

½ cup water

½ cup whole milk

1 tablespoon granulated sugar

¼ teaspoon kosher salt

1 tablespoon butter

1 cup flour

1 teaspoon vanilla extract

2 eggs

Neutral cooking oil, such as canola oil, for frying

15 pecan halves

Remove the pumpkin pieces from the cal solution, give them a quick rinse with running tap water, and put them in the pot. If the pumpkin is not fully covered with the syrup add a little more water (hot from the tap) until the water covers the pumpkin. Cover the pot and cook at a simmer for about 45 minutes, or until pumpkin is totally soft.

To make the churros: Put the water, milk, sugar, salt, and butter into a pot and bring it to a boil. When all of the butter has melted, stir in the flour. Turn the heat to medium and add the vanilla extract. Continue stirring until the dough is smooth and doesn't stick to the sides of the pan; this might only take about 1 minute, or it might be a little longer.

Let the dough cool for a few minutes, until it is warm to the touch but not too hot to handle (and also not so hot that it will cook the eggs when you add them in the next step).

Put the dough into the bowl of a stand mixer. Using the paddle attachment, mix on medium speed. After about 1 minute, with the mixer still running, break 1 egg into the dough. Let it mix into the dough until fully incorporated, about 1 minute more. Then repeat the process with the second egg. The dough should be totally mixed and still warm. Transfer it into a pastry bag fitted with a star tip.

Using the pastry bag, extrude the dough into approximately 4-inch-long pipes onto a baking sheet. You can draw either straight lines or curlicues, depending on your preference. Use kitchen scissors to snip the end of the dough after extruding each pipe, to get nice clean tips.

Put the sheet pan with the dough pipes in the freezer for 20 to 30 minutes, until they are stiff.

continued

Churros, continued

Preheat the oven to 200°F. You will use this to keep the churros warm after cooking.

Line a plate with several layers of paper towels. Fill a small pot or Dutch oven with 3 inches of canola oil. Heat the oil to a steady temperature of 360°F, using a candy thermometer to keep an eye on the temperature.

Remove the dough from the freezer. Add each churro to the oil and fry for about 8 minutes, until it is a rich, dark golden brown on all sides. You can fry several at a time, depending on the size of your pot; just make sure that you don't put so many in at once that the temperature of the oil dips below 350°F.

When you remove each churro from the pot, set it on the paper towel–lined plate, to wick away excess oil. After each churro has sat for about 1 minute, transfer it to the oven (you can set them directly on the oven rack) to keep warm until serving.

Chop the pecans into small bits.

On each plate, put a scoop or two of ice cream. Then lay down an equal portion of churros on each plate so they rest against the ice cream. Pull the pumpkin slices from their pot and lay them beside the churros. Sprinkle the pumpkin pieces with the pecan bits. Spoon some extra syrup from the pumpkin pot over the whole dish and serve.

4

THE ROAD BACK HOME

On Saturday and Sunday mornings, where a dirt road meets the rural highway across from an auto parts store in the town of Guadalupe, you may see a mustachioed man tending to a large pot of pork, while local farmers and their families gather around picnic tables. That man is Rafael Magaña, chef de cuisine of Laja, who often spends his weekends manning the carnitas stand opened by his parents a couple decades back. If you come to the Valle for a weekend, this is a great stop on your way out of town. You might even be served breakfast made by the same cook who made your Michelin-caliber tasting menu the night before.

Carnitas for four

1 pound lard, plus any trimmed fat from the pork shoulder

1 pound pork shoulder, cut into 5 to 10 pieces, large fat deposits trimmed off

One 12-ounce bottle Mexican Coca-Cola

For serving

12 corn tortillas (see page 142) or flour tortillas (see page 38)

1 white onion, peeled and finely chopped

½ bunch cilantro, chopped, stem bases removed

Pico de Gallo (page 133)

Tangy Red Salsa (page 136)

In Mexico, particularly in the state of Michoacán, carnitas—pork cooked slowly in its own fat—is a little bit like French confit. This contrasts with carnitas in the United States, which often consists of roasted pork, pulled and then crisped on a griddle. To make the carnitas dish that we eat here, the key is to slow-cook the meat in its own fat (along with a little extra fat) after it's been briefly deep-fried in the same pot.

Melt the lard and trimmed fat over low heat in a Dutch oven or large pot. Turn the heat to high and wait 5 minutes. If the lard begins to smoke, lower the heat slightly until it stops. Add the pork shoulder one piece at a time, giving the fat time to recover its heat before adding the next piece. Stir as necessary to keep the meat cooking evenly. After the last piece of meat is added, cook for 5 to 10 minutes more, stirring as needed, until all the pieces are nicely browned. Add the Coca-Cola and turn the heat to medium-low. Cook for 1 to 2 hours more, until the meat is totally cooked and soft.

Remove the meat from the pot and put it on a large serving plate. Serve alongside the tortillas, onion, cilantro, pico de gallo, and salsa.

Carnitas for three hundred

75 pounds lard

150 pounds whole pig
(loins removed)

Six 12-ounce bottles,
Mexican Coca-Cola

6 cups kosher salt

For serving

600 corn tortillas (see page 142)
or flour tortillas (see page 38)

36 white onions, peeled and
coarsely chopped

18 bunches cilantro,
coarsely chopped

10 gallons Pico de Gallo
(page 133)

5 gallons Tangy Red Salsa
(page 136)

60 limes, cut into eighths

Sometimes a recipe for eight or even a dozen people won't cut it. The next time you find yourself in charge of throwing a big party, or when your extended family, and all their extended families, are coming over on a Sunday—well, here's how you can feed them, Baja wine country–style.

Visit your local pig farmer and offer to buy a whole pig, except for the loins. The loins are the cut where pork chops come from; those will sell for a lot more money than the rest of the pig and they're not really great for carnitas anyway. You can use everything else from the animal that comes from the processor—all the slow-cooking cuts, of course, and also all the trim (tell them you'd like it just as trim, not made into sausage), the offal, even the skin if they do that. You'll likely end up with about 150 pounds of pig.

You'll also need a cooking vessel for the carnitas. The pot that is used for this purpose is called a *cazo*, it's shaped kind of like a large, squat version of the cone that a dog wears around its head after going to the vet, but with a bottom. Traditionally a *cazo* is made of copper, but you can also buy it in steel. You're going to need a very big one, or maybe two. (See "Specialty Cookware," page 253, for suggestions on procuring them.) You can get by with a little less cooking capacity if you cook the pig in two batches over a couple days—refrigerate the first batch, and then reheat it at serving time. Cooking in multiple batches is quite common in carnitas restaurants—just make sure you maintain the theater of having the second pot still cooking for your guests to watch, even while you are serving the first! You will also need a large paddle to stir the hot meat. The traditional wooden carnitas-stirring paddle is called a *pala*. Again, see page 253 for tips on where to procure one. I suppose a wooden oar from your local rowing club would work in a pinch.

Note: If you received the pig whole or in parts too big to fit in your pot, break it down into manageable sizes. Separate the skin, large pieces of fat, and meat.

Make a fire pit, surrounded by about fifty bricks arranged in a shape that will support the cooking vessel as it sits over the fire.

Start the fire. Put the lard and the butchered pig fat in the pot over the fire. It will melt and then start bubbling. Then it will stop bubbling. Drop a piece of meat in the fat; if the fat is so hot that the meat fries, it's ready.

Put the meat into the fat, bit by bit. Use your paddle to stir the pot so nothing sticks to the bottom. The meat should brown from the hot fat. One all the meat is well browned, add the Coca-Cola to the pot, which will have the effect of cooling down the pot to a less crispy-making temperature. Adjust the fire as necessary to keep the heat steady but moderate—our goal is to cook the pork all the way through over a couple of hours without burning the outside. Cook for 1 hour, adding 1½ cups salt every 15 minutes or so. As you add the last batch of salt, taste a little bit of the pork (find an edge that is fully cooked) to verify that you have the amount of salt to your taste. Cook for another 30 minutes. Add the skin if you have it. Cook for 40 minutes more.

The meat is ready when it falls easily off the bone. If it's not there yet, keep cooking until it is. The whole cooking process can take as long as 5 hours depending on the size of everything and the heat level; most of the time, it will be more like 2 or 3 hours.

When the meat is done, remove it from the pot. Serve alongside the tortillas, onions, cilantro, pico de gallo, salsa, and lime wedges.

PURCHASING NOTES

For most people in the United States, the easiest place to find many of the distinctly Mexican items in this book is the closest neighborhood or village where there's a sizable population of Mexican immigrants and their families. Very likely there's a community like this in your city or somewhere close to it. You're likely to find at least one market with a good selection of chiles, canned ingredients, corn husks for tamales, prepared foods such as *masa harina* and *chicharrones*, and probably the best mass-market tortillas available locally. They're also likely to have some specialty kitchen implements, like tortilla presses and *palas*.

In that same neighborhood you might also find an indie tortilleria, or a large grocery store with its own tortilla-making facility, offering not just fresh-made corn tortillas but also *masa para tortillas*. And there might be also be a cookwares shop (or, once again, a comparable section in a large Latino grocery store) that offers larger and more niche equipment, like *cazos*, paella pans, and hand grinders for nixtamal.

Additionally, in these areas, you may be able to find—either in grocery stores or standing alone—butchers who break down whole animals in the way that was common throughout the United States a couple of generations ago. From them, it will be possible to get specialty cuts of meat such as pork jowl. The supply chains that stock these butchers are often quite antiquated and thus a bit more wholesome than the most modern producers. However, if you specifically want to use pastured meats—which I recommend if you can swing it—you'll probably have to befriend a local artisanal butcher or, at the very least, the meat counter at a gourmet grocer.

Similarly, in most of the United States, the quality of seafood you'll want in order to fully enjoy the recipes in the book is beyond what's available at chain grocery stores. I suggest visiting your local seafood shops and talking with them about what they have, what they can get, and what's the best quality. Also, you may have access to a community supported fishery, or "CSF," subscription in your area; that is often the best and most affordable way to get seafood of the quality we in Baja are used to. You can subscribe to your local CSF, and on the weeks where they give you something that's in this book, like crab or halibut, whip up that recipe and impress your friends and family with your talent!

Finally, there is at least one brick-and-mortar location that is accessible to millions of Americans, offers a lot of the pantry goods in this book, such as chiles and herbs, and has an extensive selection of Mexican cookware and equipment. That place is Mercado Hidalgo in Tijuana; this small shopping center is the border city's historic central market. Returning across the border can be subject to delays depending on the time of day and other factors, but the market is very easy to reach. It's less than two miles from the border crossing and makes for a fun shopping excursion. Plus, there is an amazing taco stand right outside, called Tacos Fito; I recommend you check it out.

Now, some people won't be able to access some or any of the mentioned vendors; others will want to track down some very niche items such as specific varieties of heirloom foods. For these reasons and more, here we list some remote resources that might be helpful.

Beans

Rancho Gordo, the granddaddy of heirloom bean boutiques in the United States, continues to serve as the go-to vendor for specialty beans from all of the Americas, along with many other products. You can make purchases online at ranchogordo.com, find their products at select retailers, or go to their store in Napa, California.

Rancho Llano Seco, outside of Chico, dates back to a land grant from when that part of California was in Mexico. This company is well-known in the Bay Area for its pork but also has an excellent selection of estate-grown heirloom beans. Their online store is at llanoseco.com.

Pinquito beans, whose Spanglish name translates to the accurate description "like pink beans but smaller," are said to be native to the Central Coast of California, near Santa Maria. The beans are still widely available in Santa Maria, and you can buy them online from the Righetti family at **Susie-Q's** (susieqbrand.com).

Corn for Nixtamal

As the interest in pre-Hispanic cuisine has grown, so has the availability of dried corn kernels well-suited for nixtamalization. An online search will probably turn up multiple options convenient for you. That said, **Anson Mills** has been selling this kind of corn, which they call "hominy corn," north of the border for longer than anyone we know. Founder Glenn Roberts grew up near the Baja border where his family dry-farmed grains in Jacumba; now he traffics in antebellum varieties of grain identified in the Southeast United States. Purchase Anson Mills products at ansonmills.com.

Dried Chiles and *Carne Seca*

Numerous purveyors of Mexican specialties have an online presence, and, of course, many are also aggregated by the online retail giants. These purveyors tend to have a wide selection of dried foods, including chiles, spices, and sometimes *carne seca*. Your best bet is to do an Internet search to find the latest information on what's what.

Sushi-Grade Fish and Shellfish

Most of the specialty seafood in this book can be purchased, when in season, from San Diego's **Catalina Offshore Products**. Catalina deals directly with seafood receivers in Baja and, in many cases, is shipping the same product that we are eating in Ensenada. Additionally, their sea urchin—sourced from both San Diego and Baja—has long been the choice of many of California's highest-end restaurants. Catalina's online shop is at catalinaop.com.

In U.S. California, wild-harvested abalone can't be sold legally, but a handful of abalone farms exist on either side of the border. In the United States, you can order farm-direct from **American Abalone Farms** in Monterey Bay at americanabalone.com.

Cal (culinary lime)

In the United States, cal is sold at select small Mexican markets and at most large Latino supermarkets. Even at stores that carry cal, it can be hard to locate. At smaller markets, you might find it in the display rack featuring small bags of spices and dried chiles. Usually you'll have to ask someone working at the store where it is; you may well have to ask several people. If you can't track down any cal in person, you can easily find it online. All the big guys have it—search for "cal Mexicana" or "pickling lime"—and you also can buy it from **Anson Mills**, where it's called "culinary lime," at ansonmills.com.

Specialty Cookware

If you want a specific piece of cookware and you strike out locally, your best bet is to search online. Here are some useful search terms for pots and pans associated with different dishes.

> **Carnitas:** *cazo*, carnitas pot, carnitas *pala* (*pala* is the name of the wooden paddle used for stirring the carnitas)
>
> **Caguamanta:** paella pan
>
> **Tortillas:** *comal* for tortillas, *plancha*, tortilla griddle
>
> **Fish Taco:** *comal pozo*, *pozo* pan. *Pozo* means "well," and this pan has a well in the center for frying the fish pieces, which you can then dry out on the skirt that is raised out of the oil.
>
> **Other Tacos:** *comal bola*. This pan is shaped opposite of the *pozo* pan; it has a raised dome (*bola*) center, which is useful for heating tortillas while stewed fillings cook in liquid on the skirt below.

ACKNOWLEDGMENTS

We (David and Jay) would like to acknowledge a deep debt of gratitude to our dear friend Jair Téllez, who, at different times and in different ways, served as a mentor to both of us and who also introduced us to each other many years ago. Jair's contributions to cuisine and culture are myriad, often underpublicized, and always compelling.

We're very appreciative of the extensive time spent with us in service of this book by our colleagues and friends Ezekiel Hernandez of De Garo Ja'Mat, Ismene Venegas of El Pinar de 3 Mujeres, Tito Cortes of Rancho Cortes, and Marcelo Ramonetti of La Cava de Marcelo. Thanks are also due to Eileen and Phil Gregory at La Villa del Valle, Javi Martinez from Boules, Lisa Skerl, Gail DiBerardinis, and Roberto Gallegos for their very active help and support on this project.

The contents of this book reflect the contributions of many cooks, chefs, culinarians, producers, makers, and artists, including some who are named in the main text and many who are not. We could not have put it together without them. These contributors include, but are by no means limited to, Alejandro D'Acosta, Hugo D'Acosta, Lucas D'Acosta, Roberto Alcocer, Benito Altamira, Andres Blanco, Derrik Chinn, Drew Deckman, Angela Ferrer, Pablo Ferrer, Miguel Angel Guerrero, Diego Hernandez, Hector Herrera, Rafael Magaña, David Martinez, Lulu Martinez, Benito Molina, Solange Muris, Rebeca Ojeda, Paolo Paoloni, Pau Pijoan, Javier Plascencia, Rosendo Ramos, Eugenio Romero, Rosi Saldaña, Ryan Steyn, Claudia Turrent, and Tim Yarbrough.

We are very grateful to the entire team at Fauna for their work in support of this book; and also for creating a destination that is full of joy and good food.

The folks at Ten Speed Press made this book possible: Emily Timberlake initiated it; Kelly Snowden shaped it; Dervla Kelly edited it; Emma Campion and Mari Gill designed it; and along with Kaitlin Ketchum introduced us to photographer Oriana Koren; Amy Bauman copyedited it; Enrique Ciapara drew the maps; Jane Chinn served as production manager; and Doug Ogan served as managing editor. Our photography team comprised Oriana, food stylist Jillian Knox, and Yasara Gunawardena. It's a gift to have partnered with all of these folks and surely others who worked on the book without us meeting them.

Thanks, of course, to Maribel, for everything.

Most important, we need to acknowledge the many cooks, farmers, fishermen/fisherwomen, and laborers who we know only by way of the delicious food through which they've nourished us, for days and months and years, up and down the peninsula, in both Californias, and beyond. Thank you.

INDEX

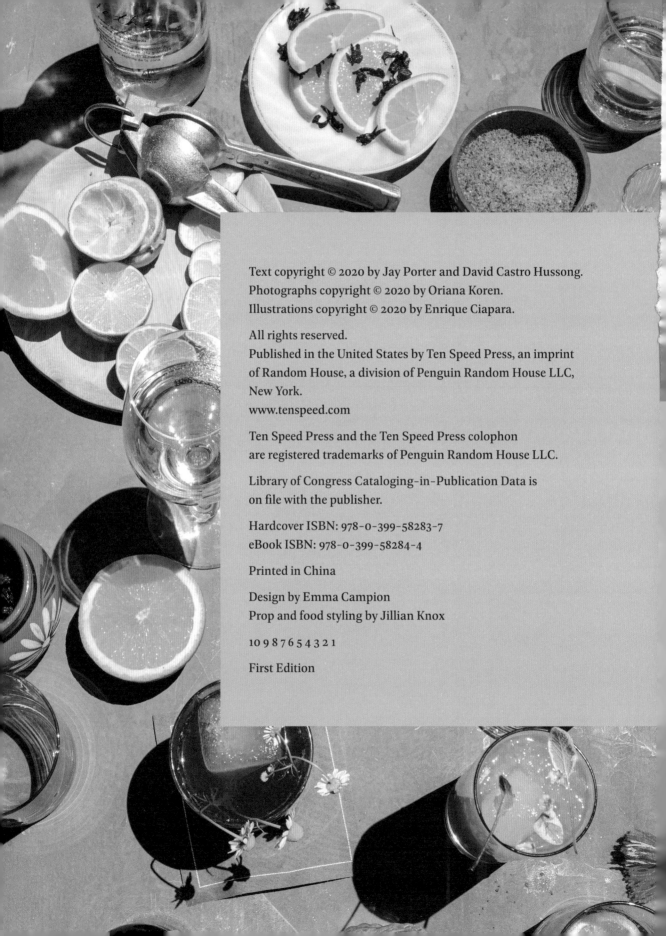

Text copyright © 2020 by Jay Porter and David Castro Hussong.
Photographs copyright © 2020 by Oriana Koren.
Illustrations copyright © 2020 by Enrique Ciapara.

Published in the United States by Ten Speed Press, an imprint
of Random House, a division of Penguin Random House LLC,
New York.
www.tenspeed.com

Ten Speed Press and the Ten Speed Press colophon
are registered trademarks of Penguin Random House LLC.

Library of Congress Cataloging-in-Publication Data is
on file with the publisher.

Hardcover ISBN: 978-0-399-58283-7
eBook ISBN: 978-0-399-58284-4

Printed in China

Design by Emma Campion
Prop and food styling by Jillian Knox

10 9 8 7 6 5 4 3 2 1

First Edition